From Together To Triumph

Five Couples' Journey To Extraordinary Success

Robert Shelton

Robert Shelton/Axio Publishing
1145 S 800 E Suite 100
Orem, UT/84097
www.axiowm.com

Publisher's Note: This book and the content provided herein are simply for educational purposes and do not take the place of professional advice. Every effort has been made to ensure that the content provided in this book is accurate and helpful for our readers at publishing time. However, this is not an exhaustive treatment of the subjects. No liability is assumed for losses or damages due to the information provided.

From Together To Triumph/Robert Shelton -- 1st ed.
ISBN 979-8-9851359-2-3

To my amazing wife, Melissa. Your unwavering strength and wisdom have been the foundation of our success - with your forgiveness lighting our path through every misstep and challenge. In the sanctuary of your love, I've found the courage and integrity to chase our dreams together. This book, a testament to our journey, is dedicated to you. All my love, Rob

"The best way to love someone is to help them reveal the greatest version of themselves."

—UNKNOWN

Contents

Acknowledgements

This book stands as a bridge between dreams and reality, a journey through the lives of five incredible couples who have graciously shared their stories of love, struggle, and success. Their openness and honesty have not only enriched these pages but have also illuminated the path for others to follow. It is with profound gratitude that I extend my heartfelt thanks to each amazing couple for entrusting me with their narratives and allowing us to learn from their experiences.

I am deeply indebted to my editor, whose keen insights and unwavering patience helped shape this work into its final form. Your dedication and creativity with the production team have brought the essence of these stories to life in a way that words alone could not convey. Your collective talents have been indispensable in bringing this project to fruition.

To my friends and colleagues, who have offered their encouragement and support throughout this journey, your belief in this project has been a source of constant motivation. Your constructive feedback and spirited discussions have been invaluable, refining my thoughts and directing my focus where it was needed most.

At the core of this endeavor, and indeed my life, is my incredible wife, Melissa. Your spirit permeates every page of this book, your resilience inspires every story, and your love is the thread that binds this entire endeavor together. I am truly blessed that we navigate the waters of life with love and laughter, and our children, who have been an integral part of our success, continually add joy, purpose, and perspective to our journey.

Lastly, to you, the reader, who has embarked on this journey with us, thank you. May the stories within these pages inspire you, challenge you, and encourage you to chase your dreams with the same fervor and dedication. May it help empower you to unlock the freedom to live your best life!

Introduction

How do you define success?

Chances are –your definition of success is as personal to who you are as your definition of happiness, or love. In each of these cases, how these terms are defined is as unique as the individuals defining them.

According to Miriam-Webster, success in its most basic form can be defined as, "the accomplishment of an aim or purpose." When you ask most people how they define success, they'll typically respond with some version of, "being able to pay the bills and provide for their family – maybe have a cushy savings account or if they're an entrepreneur, providing benefits for their employees."

I am lucky enough to be in one of the most amazing businesses in the world. As a financial advisor[1], I have

---

[1] Securities offered through J.W. Cole Financial, Inc (JWC) Member FINRA/SIPC. Advisory services offered through J.W. Advisors, Inc. (JWCA). JWC, JWCA and Axio Wealth Management are unaffiliated entities. The views and opinions expressed herein are those of the Robert Shelton and do not necessarily reflect the views or positions of JWC, JWCA or Axio Wealth Management.

met and continue to meet remarkably successful entrepreneurs from all walks of life. The more I got to know them, the more I realized that these self-made individuals defined success very differently relative to traditional views.

This is a book about success and the paths that five very different couples took to get there – the challenges they had to overcome and the lessons they learned about life, each other, and themselves along the way. What I found particularly interesting was the degree to which their definitions of success broadened and evolved as they reached new pinnacles of success.

I stress the word, "couple" here, in the beginning and throughout the book because this isn't just a book about the entrepreneur of the story. In each of our couple's stories, one spouse provided for the family as the primary breadwinner while the other spouse stayed at home and provided for the family and home in an equally important role.

In four of our five stories, roles and responsibilities fell along traditional lines with the wife staying at home to take care of the family and the husband working outside the home. However, in the Petersen's story, you'll discover that this couple chose to throw tradition out the window when it made more sense for their family. In their case, it was hard-driving, dirt bike-riding, Jeff who stayed at home with the kids while Karen provided for the family in her high-powered job outside of the home.

Yes, this is a book about success, but this book is different because it provides equal time to the often unsung hero in many entrepreneurial success stories – the rock and foundation behind the scenes – the spouse. In my own journey, I am the first to recognize that there's no way I could have accomplished what I have professionally had I not had the unwavering support of my wife.

In this book, we honor not just the talent of entrepreneurs. In this book, we honor the essential and pivotal role that supportive spouses play in entrepreneurial stories everywhere across the country.

For this is not an easy role. In business, many of an entrepreneur's decisions are clearcut and analytical in nature. That is rarely the case for the spouse at home balancing children, repairmen, adolescents, school, sports and all the emotions that go along with those.

Virtually every couple in this book recognized early in their journey the importance of positive self-care and strong mental health. Each of our couples found strength and guidance through their faith and many also sought out counseling in areas such as communication, conflict resolution and to heal past issues and move forward.

Although society may have only recently released the stigma associated with seeking help in mental health areas, our couples don't hesitate to credit mental health counseling and positive self-care as key components in their success. Invariably, it helped everyone involved communicate better and handle conflict more effectively with their spouse, their family in business interactions as well.

Each couple has intriguing stories to tell and lessons to teach. I encourage you to *treat* yourself to this book – take your time with it and savor it – for the lessons in these pages extend far beyond just success and financial gain. There are lessons of life, perspective, family and faith within these pages.

Part 1

Paul and
Rachel Adams

Chapter 1

Paul and Rachel Adams Backstory

We all experience crossroads in our lives – those pivotal points when a single decision defines the very trajectory of our life - or at least our direction for years to come. The interesting thing about Paul Adams is the crossroads in his life began before he was even born.

I've known Paul for most of my life – since 7th grade to be exact and to say he started life on shaky ground would be an understatement. Paul was to be his mother's fourth child. However, due to her poor circumstances, and the unfortunate situation she was in, she decided early in her pregnancy that she would pursue adoption to give Paul a better shot at life.

Everything was in place and the stage was set for Paul to be adopted. His adoptive parents were present for his birth but at the last minute, torn with indecision, Paul's mother changed her mind. To hear Paul tell it – "she had an extremely tough choice to make. Being adopted herself, with many different homes and foster families in her past, I'm sure this wasn't an easy decision for anyone to make in that situation."

It wasn't exactly a fairy tale ending either. Baby boy arrives home to a very cramped home with three other kids and an abusive boyfriend.

Fortunately for Paul, the man who was supposed to be his adoptive dad and had a strong love, and compassion for his friend – a single mom, as well as all of the kids involved – found a way to continue to visit on a regular basis. For the next several years, he witnessed the nightmare scenario the boy lived in and called home. To Paul, he became affectionately known as Uncle Dave.

When Paul was 4 years old, the situation became so dire that the current arrangement had to end. Dave stepped in and offered to adopt Paul. After coming to an agreement with his mother, he asked Paul if he wanted to live with him. Paul grinned and stuffed everything he owned into a single black garbage bag, and he was off with his new family to McDonald's.

According to Paul's adoptive mom, he sat in the car – happy as a clam as they drove to his new home. At the age of four, Paul had already experienced two major crossroads in his short life. He never asked about or mentioned his family again.

His siblings? They are mothers, fathers, cancer survivors, craftsmen, and business owners. All are high contributing members of society, and "incredible people" as Paul so affectionately calls them.

Paul grew up in a middle-class, hard-working family. Both of his parents were insurance agents and although they lived modestly, he always knew he was loved. He didn't exactly excel in school but maintained a solid 2.6 gpa – only because that was the minimum required to stay on the wrestling team.

His next crossroads would come when he was 14 years old and met a very special girl at a family reunion. Sparks flew and emotions ran high. That girl was Rachel. Paul loves watching the concerned expression on faces when he tells people that he met his wife at a family reunion - and the subsequent relief when he shares that he was adopted!

They would see each other every couple of years at family events but Paul always knew she was the one. The couple was married right after high school. They didn't exactly have a life plan so Paul's dad started pressing him to get his insurance license so he could take over his agency one day.

Paul knew the insurance business wasn't for him but like most good teenage kids, he lied and said he'd get licensed - only so he could play on the office computer. His dad felt it was important that he learn to interact with people effectively — look them in the eye, a firm handshake, Business 101 stuff — so he had Paul start dropping off checks and bills to clients.

It just so happened that one the places Paul visited was a web development firm. It was the early 2000s and when he dropped off the bill, all the programmers were in one big room hard at work building small websites going for $20,000 apiece. Paul was immediately intrigued and hooked. His daily routine became drop off the bill, pick up the check and then spend a couple of hours loitering and learning.

First, he built his dad a website and Paul will be the first to admit it was pretty bad by today's standards but then he started doing graphic presentations for his dad to use with clients. It wasn't long before clients started asking him to do the same for their companies. Clients soon started dropping the checks off to Paul and that's when his business career really began.

His dad never stopped asking about the status of his insurance license and Paul knew it was time to spread his wings. He was ready for bigger and better things, so he and Rachel moved to California.

Ironically, Paul went to work for an insurance company - but this wasn't any insurance company. It was one of the first online insurance companies. This was Paul's first taste of online marketing. The company partnered with eBay, Edmunds.com and other online giants. Paul was mentored by people on the cutting edge of online marketing.

He continued to grow in his position and the time came when he knew it was time to move on to other new startups. Because Utah is fertile ground for startups, he moved back to Utah and found a job with a new startup. Paul continued to strategically place himself in the company of smart tech people and refers to this time as his "free tuition" period.

He watched some startups take off and others explode. Soon, he felt he was ready to go out on his own and start his first consulting business. Unfortunately, his timing wasn't the greatest. 2008 hit and took the entire economy down with it.

Paul started calling everyone he knew, trying to convince them that he could get them more online leads than they were getting internally. One day, he was talking to a sales rep who put him in touch with some people out in Los Angeles who were looking for online leads. They connected and became one of Paul's first customers.

He started doing consulting for them and from there, started his consulting agency - Skyrocket. Paul did online marketing and conversion optimization, and the company grew rapidly. A couple of people approached Paul about partnering so Skyrocket would have the capital necessary to grow into a formidable company doing real things in a real office.

Skyrocket Consulting became Skyrocket Media, and the partners complimented each other well. The company expanded into building web properties designed to drive customers to other businesses and the company continued to grow almost exponentially. In 2 years, the company experienced a growth rate of approximately 8000%.

You'll soon discover in the next chapter that Paul is an entrepreneur's entrepreneur. He's happiest when he's pushing and hustling. He's not one to stand still and he's never content with the status quo. His ideas for moving the company forward were perceived by his partners as radical and too risky. Paul explains what happened next as a "misalignment" with his partners.

Paul arrived at the office and what started as an ordinary day soon became anything but. It would become a day that Paul would never forget. His partners met with him and informed him that they planned to enforce a provision in the operating agreement — a forced buyout of his third of the company.

Paul was stunned. He and Rachel had poured their heart and soul into the company. They'd pulled many an all-nighter building Paul's dream from the ground up and now it was being taken away from them. This was an extremely difficult time for the couple but as you'll discover in the next two chapters, they relied heavily on their faith and each other to get through.

What impressed me most about this time in Paul's life is he kept it professional and amicable. He never allowed himself to become negative about his partners. When I was interviewing him for the book, he explained it this way − "If Rachel and I were walking through the jungle with a bag of oranges and we lost half our oranges, some people would cry and give up, other people would spend all their time looking for the lost oranges, but we would decide to go look for a new orange tree."

And − that's exactly what they did. Paul took a couple of days to process his loss but then all his time and effort went into developing his next business idea. His first idea didn't pan out, but he was undeterred. Although he didn't know it at the time, his next crossroad was just around the corner.

He received a call from his first consulting clients out in California and they were doing a new startup for invisible braces that they called Byte, and they wanted him to be a part of it. At first, Paul wasn't real interested but his former clients were so enthusiastic about the idea, he continued to listen and ask questions. Paul asked about their web address and when he found out that it was byteme.com, he was in.

Paul and Rachel will tell you that what they thought was their darkest days − being forced out of Skyrocket, turned out to be their greatest blessing. Paul and his partners bootstrapped Byte and built it up for two years. Then they sold the company for over $1Billion!

What strikes me most about Paul is that even when faced with the most devastating blow in his professional life, he never burned bridges or became vindictive. In fact, Byte even did business with his old company. Paul is a master at relationships – targeting them, building them, nurturing them, and leveraging them.

What impresses me about Rachel in all of this is her ability to always choose happiness and look for that silver lining in every situation. According to Paul, "She is that sprinkling of ingredients that makes me better." Rachel has always played an integral role in Paul's success. She is not just his wife - he considers her his Vice-President of Everything.

You have their backstory. Now it's time to meet Paul and   Rachel   personally.

Chapter 2

Paul Adams
Perspective

"When you're grateful, you are invincible."

Paul Adams

Great life lessons are gifts. However, sometimes these gifts come wrapped in our biggest mistakes. When Paul and I talked about lessons and mistakes on his amazing journey to success, his comments on each were both immediate and identical. Rachel, Rachel, Rachel!

Looking back on his professional life, Paul admits that one of the biggest mistakes he made was not relying on

Rachel sooner. He spent years building his career without her help or opinion.

He viewed her primary role as taking care of the kids. After all, they have seven children and at one point, all seven were under the age of 11. Recognizing that this alone was a full-time job, he only discussed things with her and asked for her opinion when things were not going well.

Rachel always found a way to help him figure out potential solutions. Her belief in Paul was and remains unshakable. She knew he was capable of great things and believed with every fiber of her being that he could do anything - even when he wasn't so sure.

Rachel became Paul's confidence coach, and it became glaringly obvious to him that he'd left his best player on the bench far too long. When he was navigating the business world, he was out for himself as self-preservation and because of his drive to rise to the top. Paul realized that Rachel was the only player in the game who was out there for "them." And, because she wasn't in his business world, her primary concern was what was best for the well-being of their family.

Paul began to view Rachel as his business partner and together, they are a powerful team both on and off the business field. He discusses all issues and opportunities with her. She is his sounding board, and they make business decisions together. Whenever Paul is asked about lessons learned, and he gets asked that a lot these days, he's quick to answer unequivocally, "Make your spouse your business partner."

Faith Moves Mountains

Paul and Rachel are deeply spiritual people, and their faith is an integral part of who they are. They are quick to point out that God has always been the senior partner on their team. Even so, it hasn't always been easy for this successful couple.

When they moved out to California and Paul took the job with a big online insurance company, money was tight. They won't ever forget those times when even after paying only $850 in rent for their cramped apartment, they still came up short every month. They ended up having to see their bishop for food assistance to feed their family.

Regardless of the obstacles they faced, they never expected quick fixes. They trusted that nothing happened to them – it was all happening for them. Rachel prayed for Paul's work every day.

Paul laughs when he recalls how he would just pray that things would work out – but not Rachel. Her prayers were always very specific. She prayed that God would help Paul change the metrics of the entire company - and her prayers were answered.

Paul won the Star Award – a highly coveted honor that was only given to one out of 250 employees. Rachel was so proud of him that night, but even prouder when they announced that he'd won the award for "changing the metrics of the company!"

Every day they read the Book of Mormon and every day they sharpened their ax. To this day, Paul relies on his spiritual intuition to guide him in making his next right decision. However, this doesn't mean that he hasn't made some mistakes along the way. He just trusts that everything is building for his good.

While working for the company in Californica, Paul made a critical mistake. He inadvertently had the wrong phone number printed on 500 catalogs for a company that generated 80% of its revenue from catalog sales. They had two kids at the time and Paul was in a panic when he called Rachel.

After explaining to her what had happened, he told her that he knew he was going to lose his job, or he would have to quit. Unflappable, Rachel listened and then calmly said that she was going to pray about it. She told Paul to say a prayer wherever he could and then call her back.

Paul said his prayer and not quite sure what to expect, he dialed his wife back. She answered quickly and told him that she felt calm about Paul quitting and that everything was going to be okay. He quit his job that day and the family moved back to Utah.

Paul is a strong believer in the Japanese business philosophy of Kaizen which emphasizes continual movement forward and gradual, methodical improvement. He quickly adds that continuous movement forward is much easier when you have someone you can count on who is with you. So, move forward they did.

Paul has said that "the mind is most fertile after a mistake." That's when your mind is most open to new ideas and different approaches. When he started his new consulting business in Utah, he took a bold and definitely different approach.

As mentioned in the previous chapter, Paul started his new consulting business right before the Great Recession of 2008. They hit hard times and almost lost their home, but their faith never wavered and with Rachel's help, Paul kept pushing. During this time, he never dreamed of luxuries like a fancy car - he just wanted to put food on the table and not have to ask the bishop for another food order.

He called everyone he knew and when someone would call to talk about a contract, he would tell them that he was already booked. He was confident he could bring in more leads than they were getting from their internal marketing team, and they knew it too. They'd invariably call back and beg him to come out and talk to them.

When he landed his first big client, he was working from his living room but he set up company emails for all his kids so the company looked much bigger than it was. He frequently included clients in an email thread between himself and one of the fictitious emails, requesting that person provide something to the client – essentially exchanging emails with himself.

It worked and Skyrocket was born. Paul essentially did everything, and the company grew. Both Paul and

Rachel believed that God was in everything every step of the way – every company, every person, and every opportunity.

When his partners forced the buyout against Paul, the couple was devastated. This was their baby and now it was being snatched away from them. Again, they relied on their faith, each other, and their senior partner, God to pull them through what seemed to them to be the darkest of days.

Paul showed his strength and integrity throughout the situation. He was hurt – no doubt - but he remained positive toward his former partners and looked for new ways to leverage those relationships.

Now, looking back on it, Paul and Rachel realize that everything was happening for their good. Their darkest days turned out to be their greatest blessing. If the forced buyout hadn't occurred, Paul would not have been a part of the new startup, Byte, which turned out to be successful beyond what either could have ever imagined.

Money And Success Lessons From Dad

When I asked Paul what lessons he hoped to pass along to his kids about money and success, his answers may surprise you. The most important concept he said he wanted them to understand was that money does not equal success.

When you have love in your life, that is success. It doesn't come from anywhere outside of you – nothing material or physical can give it to you. You can have all the money in the world and still not feel successful within yourself.

Your outlook is your success. It is your perspective that drives your performance and ultimately your journey to success. Your ability to move through obstacles and do what needs to be done largely depends on your perspective. Your ability to get knocked down but not stay down – your ability to get back up and not be jaded – that is success.

His advice to his kids would be to learn to enjoy all the things that money can't buy. Then, when they acquire all the cool material things that money can buy – they can enjoy them with the confidence that if all material things disappeared tomorrow, they would still be happy. That is true success.

Paul remembers one of the happiest times in his life as sitting on the floor in that cramped apartment in California on the cheap carpet playing with his kids. He had nothing material to his name, but he was happy and that was success.

He would encourage his kids to never put limits on themselves. The only limitations we have are the ones we give ourselves. Put your subconscious to work for you. Visualize how you want everything to go before it happens. Don't put a date on it but visualize with all five of your senses to make it real. Then the question becomes, can your subconscious dream big enough for all you're capable of?

Finally, Paul wants to instill in his children the lesson of gratitude. Be grateful for everything. His quote to start this chapter helped him on his success journey - "When you're grateful, you are invincible." It got him through the challenges and dark times. You can always find something to be grateful for. If your outlook is your success, you can count on gratitude to always keep it positive.

Hindsight

It is said that hindsight is an exact science. If Paul could go back and change anything on his journey, what would he change? When I asked him that, he stared out the window for a long time before answering.

He smiled and said that he would have spent more time enjoying his kids. Paul has always been an involved dad but looking back he wishes he had taken a little more time to enjoy them while they were young and sweet. They grow up so fast – it all goes by in a blink.

He also would not have taken things so personally. Anything anyone says or does to you is really just a projection of the world in which they live. He would have trusted his gut and spiritual intuition more, and his wife sooner.

Paul is an inspiration to everyone who knows him. Who knows what the future holds for him? Whatever it is, he'll attack it with limitless energy and he's unstoppable with Rachel at his side. Now let's meet this amazing   woman.

Chapter 3

Rachel Adams
Faith

"Success is for everyone."

Rachel Adams

R achel came from humble beginnings. Her family never had wealth and she grew up with hard-working parents who instilled a strong work ethic in their daughter.

Rachel's parents never shielded her from anything hard. She worked in the family business and struggled along with her parents and siblings. She worked long hours and often finished the day bone tired from working so hard, but her parents needed everyone to contribute.

She did what was expected of her, but Rachel knew this was not the life she wanted for herself – poor and working desperately hard. It was feelings of gratitude that got her through those hard times. She forced herself to look for the good and embrace it in every situation. Instead of resenting having to contribute, she turned it around and focused on being grateful that she could contribute.

When Rachel was young, a family tragedy would forever change the lens through which she saw the world. Her 3-year-old baby brother drowned. Everyone loved him so much and the entire family was devastated. At that moment, Rachel realized that it was relationships that mattered more than anything else in life.

Losing a child is one of the hardest things anyone can ever face in life. Her parents had a choice. They could wallow in self-pity but instead, Rachel saw their capacity to cope enlarged by their faith, and her faith grew as well.

One of Rachel's superpowers is staying positive in all situations. Knowing who you are gives you a certain resilience and Rachel has always known who she is.

Lessons Learned

Paul is a very lucky man to have had Rachel by his side since he was 14 years old. Her faith is built on solid rock and has weathered all the storms they have endured on their journey to success unscathed. Rachel is proud of her faith, and she goes there first every day in good times and bad.

You'll find that throughout this book a question I asked each of the couples I interviewed was what was the biggest lesson they learned on their success path? Rachel's answer was very interesting. She said she would have trusted the process sooner.

I asked her what exactly she meant by that. She said that she's learned to trust God sooner and even though she may not be able to see it at the time, everything truly is always working for their good.

She went onto explain that in many situations, we can't possibly see the big picture, but she trusts that the Lord will guide them through and to the next step every time. When they faced the forced buyout by Paul's Skyrocket partners, she felt they had done everything right. They worked hard and did everything they could to grow the company. Paul had made a lot of great decisions. He'd always been a real team player and was pro-everyone. To see that used against him was difficult for her.

However, her faith gave her the strength to do what she had to do. Divine guidance helped her find the right words to support him. Success to Rachel means peace and that was exactly what she was able to give to Paul.

Later, when they realized that their darkest hour with Skyrocket ended up being their greatest blessing through Byte, it all made sense. This has taught her and reinforced her desire to trust her spiritual process sooner.

Money and Success Lessons From Mom

When Rachel and I talked about the lessons she wanted to pass along to her kids, like Paul, the first thing she said was money does not equal success. After losing her little brother, she realized that people matter much more than money ever could.

It's relationships that determine your success and good relationships with everyone is where true success lies. It's important to Rachel that she passes this concept more than any other onto her children.

She went on to explain, "You do need money and it can do some amazing things. You can bless people in their lives. I believe that God wants everyone to be successful."

She would like her children to be abundance-minded and use the power of their mind to build that mentality. She shared that soon after they were married, Paul taped a dollar bill to the bathroom mirror and put six 0s behind it. His mind knew they would be successful long before it ever materialized in their bank account. This is the mindset she'd like to develop in her kids.

She would like her children to look for miracles and expect to see them. Paul often compares Rachel to his dad. She never expected good things from him. She expected great things from him and often asked him why he was limiting himself. She wants her children to believe they can do anything they set their mind to – even the miraculous.

Mental Health

Some of Rachel's family have battled mental health issues much of their lives. This is something that Rachel has never had to deal with, but she understands it well.

Rachel has many friends and loved ones who struggle with various mental health challenges. Yet, they have learned to manage them successfully and bring their best to their marriages and families as a result. Rachel believes that it is important that everyone takes responsibility for their bodies and their minds. After all, your physical and mental health dictates what you are able to bring to your family and to the world.

Currently, Rachel is working on her degree in human and family services. She is passionate about preventative education for families and especially marriages. So much pain and grief can be avoided that way.

Knowledge is power. There is so much information out there that is easily accessible to everyone. She and Paul are constantly reading – learning, building and are constantly trying to improve their marriage and their family dynamics. She considers Paul and her dad as great examples in this area. It is our responsibility to grow and become better every day of this amazing life.

Hindsight

When I asked Rachel if she could go back, what would she change, she was quick to answer that she wouldn't change a thing. She has loved their journey and is grateful for every experience and every lesson they've learned along the way.

She has learned to keep the Spirit with her at all times. The world can be so negative and it's easy to get caught up in the negativity of work or even family. When you turn to the Spirit in every situation, it keeps you cheerful and cheerfulness builds your faith.

Rachel believes that happiness is a choice. Choose happiness – choose joy. It gives you the energy to be scrappy and develop ingenuity through hardship. Always have something to look forward to.

Your success lies in your relationships with everyone - especially your spouse, your children and God. Remember - "Success is for everybody."

Chapter 4

Lessons Learned From Paul And Rachel

Seasoned entrepreneurs understand that success is not just about financial gain or professional accomplishments. It's about the quality of your personal relationships. Harnessing the power of faith and perspective is essential in building successful relationships – both personal and professional.

Paul and Rachel's perspective is rooted in their belief that everything happens for a reason. This outlook has helped them to stay positive and maintain a growth mindset – even during difficult times. They see challenges as opportunities for learning and growth rather than setbacks.

One of my favorite stories is the one in an earlier chapter about Paul picking oranges. The ironic thing is not too long ago, Paul was on a vacation with his family down in Arizona. He posted a picture on social media of him jumping up and snatching an orange off of an orange tree. It immediately brought back thoughts of Paul and Rachel's perspective and faith: you can sit and worry about the negative things that happen in your life, but the key is to continue moving forward and discover a new orange tree. Don't worry about that one lost orange.

Paul and Rachel's shared faith has been a guiding force throughout their relationship. They believe that their marriage is a sacred bond – one that's built upon mutual respect, love and trust. They turn to their faith for guidance and wisdom – especially when facing difficult decisions.

The couple's faith and perspective has also had a positive influence in their business dealings. As a business owner, Paul understands the importance of having a clear vision and a positive attitude. He knows that obstacles and challenges are inevitable in any business. It's how we choose to view them that determines our success.

By staying positive and grounded in their faith, this couple has been able to build successful businesses while maintaining strong relationships. Their shared perspective has helped them to focus on their goals while maintaining a sense of balance between their professional and personal lives.

I can honestly say that in my profession, I've never met a successful business owner or individual who did not have their fair share of adversity. It could be the death of a young loved one, dealing with clinical depression, living in poverty, bad dealings with business partners, growing up in a drug-influenced home or any other number of things.

The key is to have the right mindset, perspective, and faith. Remember Paul's analogy about the oranges and Rachel's wise advice that she wouldn't change a thing. Everything – all of the adversity – it all shaped who they are today.

In conclusion, the power of faith and perspective cannot be overstated when building successful relationships. As a business owner, it's important to remember that success is not just about financial gain but about the journey – the people you meet and the relationships you build.

In fact, as I talk to many successful individuals, the theme is the same – they place more value on their personal relationships than their financial gain. That's where they believe that true wealth lies. Paul and Rachel's story is a testament to the power of faith and perspective in achieving success in all aspects of life.

Chapter 5

Reflecting on Life's Journeys: The Crossroads of Decision and Destiny

As we bring the chapters on Paul and Rachel's inspiring journey to a close, this would be an opportune moment for us all to pause and reflect upon our own paths. The stories we've shared are more than mere narratives of triumph and resilience—they are mirrors reflecting our own personal struggles, victories, and the pivotal crossroads back to us.

I invite you to take a moment to deeply consider the following questions. Allow yourself the space to reflect on each one thoughtfully and write down your responses along with any action items that come to mind. This exercise is not just about introspection but also about identifying concrete steps that you can take to shape your own story with intention and purpose.

Let's embark upon this reflective exploration together, finding parallels, lessons, and inspiration for our own lives within the fabric of Paul and Rachel's experiences.

1. **Reflection on Personal Crossroads:**
   - Have I encountered crossroads in my life similar to Paul's early experiences?
   - How did the decisions made at those junctures shape where I am today?
2. **Considering Support Systems:**
   - Who has been my "Uncle Dave," offering support in difficult times?
   - How have I acknowledged that support in my life?

3. **Understanding of Partnership in Success:**
   - How do I involve my loved ones in my life's ambitions and challenges?
   - Can I identify ways to better integrate them as partners in my journey, as Paul did with Rachel?

4. **The Role of Faith and Resilience:**
   - In what ways has my faith or personal beliefs helped me navigate through tough times?
   - Can I recall a moment when what appeared to be a setback turned into an opportunity?

5. **Perspective on Money and Success:**
   - How do I define success and happiness?
   - What lessons would I want to pass onto others about the relationship between material wealth, personal fulfillment, and success?

Part 2

David and
Jenny Butler

Chapter 6

David & Jenny Butler Backstory

David Butler is a dreamer – always has been. He grew up in Sugarland, TX, right outside of Houston, and has been drawn to all things creative from a very young age. Although he's now known as a celebrated author, teacher and entrepreneur, his passion for writing can be traced all the way back to his childhood.

As a kid, David had a favorite art teacher in elementary school. One of the first stories he ever wrote, he wrote for her. The story was about an art teacher with a very special paintbrush that allowed her to do all kinds of magical things. She loved the story and he found great joy in writing it.

David's dad was a dentist and his mom, an interior designer. They both worked hard but they chose to spend their time off very differently. His dad was more relationship-oriented and perfectly content lying on a beach relaxing and watching the world go by. His mom, however, was always on the go. David attributes his boundless energy to his mom, and the value he places on relationships to his dad.

Faith has always been a big part of who David is. His hometown lies in Fort Bend County, TX, considered by many to be one of the most diverse counties in the entire country. Because of where he grew up, David was exposed to a wide variety of religious beliefs. In addition to all brands of Christianity, he frequently came in contact with Hindus, Muslims, and Buddhists. As a result, he developed a very open-minded spiritual perspective.

As you'll soon discover, it's part of David's nature to be interested in almost everything. When he arrived in Utah as a Brigham Young University freshman, that insatiable curiosity led him to explore a wide variety of courses. Looking back, he laughs and explains that he was simply pursuing his ADHD degree!

He fell in love with Utah, and it quickly became home. David decided to temporarily put college on pause to serve on a 2-year mission. He would meet his wife, Jenny on this mission while they both served in Korea. Jenny was immediately drawn to David's enthusiasm for life and his compassion for all people. By the time they arrived back in the States, Jenny had adopted him as a little brother, and she knew he was meant to be a permanent part of her family. Because she was older than David, she decided the best course of action would be to fix him up with her little sister.

However, the Universe obviously had other plans. One afternoon, he dropped by unannounced to see if Jenny's sister wanted to go out with him and some of his friends. When she wasn't there, he asked Jenny instead.

David knew that evening that there was something special about the girl from his mission and as they became more involved in life back home, the age difference became less of an issue to Jenny. It wasn't long before the couple was married.

David admits that they had no idea what the plan was from there, but he was okay with that. He's never been much of a goal setter so they just kind of figured it out together as they went along. As they reflect back on that time, they both agree that there is nothing they would go back and change.

Jenny went to school in Hawaii, where her mom grew up. She would tell David often that he could never really understand her or her family unless he actually spent time in Hawaii. She suggested that he look into the satellite campus - Brigham Young Hawaii. After that discussion, David admits he never really thought about it again.

You can imagine his surprise when he came home one evening and Jenny announced that he'd gotten in. Puzzled, he remembers his response as - great - but got into what exactly? She laughed and explained that she'd completed an application for him, and he'd gotten into Brigham Young Hawaii.

What could he say? Shortly thereafter, the couple moved to Hawaii. One of the biggest lessons David felt he learned during his time there was how to live a life of hospitality and put relationships first. Hawaiians are very gracious people, and they treat their guests like royalty. David wouldn't have traded his time in the Islands for anything.

While in college, David changed jobs eight times. He was always searching for a career in which he could make a difference and feel passion for. He tried everything – he got his mortgage license, an insurance license and he even auditioned for a movie. At one point, he came very close to selling Harley Davidson motorcycles. Considering he'd never ridden a motorcycle in his life, that job was a stretch, even by David's standard!

One day in his junior year, he was having lunch with a friend to discuss the possibility of starting a dental lab (classic David), when his friend started telling him about a class he was taking on the Gospel. David's ears perked up because he needed a religion class. The class was called *Teaching the Gospel*, and it was primarily for students who aspired to teach for a living. David managed to secure a spot in the class and was instantly intrigued. In his senior year, he was offered a part-time job as a teacher.

When his part-time position turned into a full-time seminary teaching job, he felt like he'd finally found something he was good at and was able to make a difference at the same time. One thing you'll learn about David is that a highly structured environment with lots of rules just isn't his thing. He enjoyed teaching but it could be a grind and it wasn't scratching the internal itch that was always with him.

Around that time, he started writing and thought that one day he might enjoy doing some public speaking. In 2010, while teaching a seminary class, David shared the story of a stonemason, John Moyle. In addition to working as a stonemason, Moyle was also a farmer. Every week for 20 years, this man would walk from Draper to the Salt Lake Temple and do his stonework on the temple.

One day while working on the farm, he was kicked by a farm animal. His leg was broken and eventually, he had to have the leg amputated. By this time, he was in his 60s but he wasn't going to let the loss of a leg interfere with his work at the temple. He crafted a leg for himself and practiced on it until he felt comfortable. When he was ready, he walked from his farm to the temple and back. John Moyle is best known for his carving of the *Holiness to the Lord, House of the Lord* on the Salt Lake Temple façade which he carved on his first trip back after the accident.

David decided he wanted to retrace John Moyle's steps and proposed the idea to his class. They were excited and thought it would be an impactful class experience to find Moyle's house and from there, walk to the temple.

Interestingly, someone else was studying the story of John Moyle at the same time David and his class were – Emily Belle Freeman. She thought retracing his steps and making the walk herself would be a wonderful way to honor this amazing man. It just so happens that Emily's son was in David's class and shared everything that they'd just learned. He told her of David's idea to have the class make the walk and suggested they do it together.

Before it was over, David and Emily had amassed about 75 people to join them on the walk. On their trek, the two realized that they had a lot in common. After the way, they started collaborating on their shared passions – the Lord, scripture, and teaching people on their spiritual journey.

The two have coauthored the books, *The Peter Potential, Maybe Today,* and *The Unexpected Deliverer.* However, they are probably best known for their *Don't Miss This* project. It started as a way to help a small group of moms become more confident in teaching scripture to their children. The idea was to send ideas out to them weekly. After some discussion, they decided the easiest way to accomplish that would be to post videos on YouTube.

People loved it and it took off beyond what either could have imagined! With over **220,000** YouTube subscribers **with over 35 million views**, it has grown into a community of people studying scripture and learning together. David has written many other books including, *Almighty: How The Most Powerful Being In The Universe Is Also Your Heavenly Father, Redeemer: Who He Is And Who He Will Always Be,* and *Spirit: The Gift That Connects You To Heaven.*

His insatiable curiosity may one day lead him in a different direction but at least for now, David has a full-time job that he loves. When he's not writing or speaking, he and Jenny have six amazing children that keep them busy.

After this small glimpse into the history of David and Jenny's success, let's meet this amazing couple. They are both interesting and inspiring.

David Butler
Relationships

"Stuff no mattah, people mattah."

David Butler

When I first started talking to David about success, he stopped me in mid-sentence and said that success was not a word that his family used a lot. He felt that its meaning has been tainted. I must have had a puzzled look on my face because he went onto explain that the word, "success" implies victory, winning, numbers – all the things that just aren't that important to David.

He prefers to use the word, "meaningful" as in meaningful pursuits and meaningful relationships. To David, everything begins and ends with relationships and it's through our relationships that we all have the capacity to do meaningful things in our lives and particularly for the people around us.

While in Hawaii, they attended a Sunday School class. One Sunday, a man in the class, when commenting on a particular scripture said in passing, "Stuff no mattah, people mattah." David immediately turned to Jenny and told her that they were stealing that. It was going to be their family and life motto from that point forward.

Their time in Hawaii really set the trajectory and mindset of putting relationships first in every aspect of their lives. The couple decided that in their family they were going to love God and love people. The specifics of what that looks like has changed over the years, but the idea has remained a constant.

The Journey

David describes his success journey or as he prefers to call it - his journey of meaningful pursuits - as "gritty" and sometimes peppered with frustration. He defined gritty as messy and not laid out in a nice, straight path. It never is and he was quick to add – nor should it be.

Frustration is often a result of reality not meeting your expectations or the way you think things should be. In your frustration, it's important to analyze how you arrived at your expectations. In actuality, you may have developed a false idea of the way things should be. Your mind creates your expectations and when you allow yourself to become frustrated with the way life should be, you miss out on the way things are. Being a man of faith, David explains that this is when you miss God in the present.

David makes the distinction between two different types of frustration. The first is a function of thinking that you're not where you should be at a specific point in time. This type of frustration is unhealthy and non-productive.

The type of frustration David feels that he has experienced on his journey, he calls "anticipatory frustration." This is when you're so excited to create something or do something meaningful but you're not quite there yet. This brand of frustration is more of a feeling that motivates you to take that next step.

He explained it as an "inspired antsiness" or "motivational dissatisfaction" that serves to remind you that you are here to do great things. Harnessed positively, it leads to the realization that you may not be exploring all of your gifts or opportunities.

Alone, David might struggle - walking the thin line between motivational dissatisfaction and outright unproductive dissatisfaction. However, Jenny has always been his positive stabilizing force. He describes his wife as "steady" and is quick to clarify that this does *not* mean boring. It means that she is very good at finding purpose with wherever they are and reminds him that they *are* there – they are experiencing life and relationships and love right now. They don't need anything else.

Jenny is not moved by life circumstances. David, on the other hand, admits that he is easily swayed by the wind. Her steadiness is not only comforting to him, but he also feels it has been a crucial component on their journey for meaning. He describes Jenny as his North Star. Without her, he says he'd likely be shipwrecked.

David has learned and been inspired by many people along the way- some he's known and some he's never met. A lesson he's learned is that it's very important that you never fall into the trap of defining your success by their journey. He describes this as a plague in our society.

He explained that because of technology, you can be inspired by business leaders, thinkers, philosophers, and athletes that you would have never had access to in the past. However, now the door is wide open for us to compare our life and journey to the life and journey of everyone else. This can leave people feeling unsuccessful, disgruntled, and cheated.

David describes himself as an old millennial and feels fortunate to have been born at the time he was. He was born in that small window of time when kids went to elementary school, middle school and high school with no phones but were still young enough to adapt to and embrace that technology when it arrived. This gave him an opportunity to live life at his own pace and on his own journey, yet still appreciate a world dominated by technology. At 17, he could have never imagined that he would be doing what he's doing now. After all, YouTube wasn't part of career day when he was a senior.

Mistakes – I've Made a Few

David believes that mistakes are gifts in disguise. Hidden within every mistake, there is a lesson. However, you have to be patient enough to look for it and open enough to accept and learn from it. On his path, he feels he either had to make that mistake back then or he would've had to make it later because the only path to learn that lesson was in making that mistake.

David often wonders about past mistakes and asks himself - what circumstances was he able to avoid as a result of a past mistake? What opportunities did he have the confidence to pursue because of a lesson from his past?

He shared the story of how he and a friend decided to start an ecommerce business together. 3D technology was just emerging, and they had an opportunity to get involved with it early. In fact, David almost left his seminary teaching to pursue it. He and his friend went to China together to meet the people and tour the factories. They were sure it would be the next big thing.

The business ended up going nowhere and they struggled and scrapped just to sell off their existing inventory. Even though the business was a bust, David loved the experience. He learned how to take an idea and run with it. He also quickly discovered why so many people with ideas never take the necessary steps to pursue them. It can be daunting!

David felt empowered by it all - analyzing the market and choosing among packaging and shipping options. The endeavor gave him confidence that he could figure anything out.

Shortly after that experience, David and Jenny started their wall decal business which was fairly successful for them. The experience from his perceived failure or mistake helped him to launch their new business.

David learned another valuable lesson. Failures increase your knowledge and experience but the most important thing they do is raise your confidence level which always leads to new opportunities.

Lessons From Dad

David hopes to instill in his kids specific lessons about success and meaningful pursuits in life. He wants them to know the importance of acquiring a balance between following dreams and being practical.

It's important to him that his kids see that their dad follows his dreams and isn't afraid to step into the unknown. You have to be willing to be uncomfortable when trying something new and embracing the experience. However, we live in the real world – a world of taxes, bottom lines, and budgets.

He wants them to understand that sacrifice is always a part of the journey. Every pursuit has a cost associated with it and often, that means sacrificing immediate gratification and what you may want to do in the present for the sake of a bigger cause.

If having a family is meaningful to them, he would like them to develop the maturity to consider all the costs associated with that pursuit. Obviously, the financial costs must be considered, but there are also mental and emotional costs associated with having a family. His hope is that they will pursue what is meaningful to them but weigh the costs before deciding to follow that dream or another one.

David wants his kids to try different things, embrace different experiences and discover what is meaningful to them. Some people have a career that is meaningful. Other people have a career to fund something that is meaningful to them. Both are okay and he's experienced plenty of each in his life.

More than anything, David hopes he's teaching his children to fill their lives with meaningful relationships. That is where they will find true success.

Hindsight

When I asked David if he could go back and change anything on their journey, he quickly answered with a unequivocal no. He smiled and explained that he has watched enough *Avengers* to know that if you change one event on the time continuum, it changes everything.

Anything he changed in the past would have had a direct effect on his present and who he is today. Although one aspect of his life might have been better, the potential cost of going back and changing anything would have been too high in his opinion.

David tells the story of one perceived failure that turned out to be a springboard to where he is today. He was sharing with a good friend of his who is also a very successful businessman that he thought it may be time to leave his seminary teaching. The friend was enthusiastic and encouraged him to jump onboard with him at Harley Davidson.

Even though he'd never ridden a motorcycle in his life, he embraced the opportunity to work with his friend. He filled out the new employee paperwork and even told the seminary that he would be leaving. Everyone was excited.

David knew that his schedule would be drastically different, but he didn't fully understand how drastic until later. When he realized that his new hours would prohibit him from coaching his son's soccer team, he decided that this was just too big of a "miss" for him. He wasn't willing to pay that cost, so he walked away – rather awkwardly he added.

He had to tell his friend he'd changed his mind and then he had to beg for his old job back. David admits the whole experience was embarrassing.

However, when he was about to leave his teaching job, he worked through the entire decision spiritually. He considered what might happen next. He'd always been drawn to teaching youth and, in a way, felt like he was abandoning his purpose. He prayed about it and weighed what God expected of him.

Through the experience, David says he learned how to make a good and comprehensive decision – one that considered all the costs. He says that had he not done his spiritual work then, he would not have had the confidence and wisdom to make that decision 6-7 years later.

He concluded that even through all the things he tried and didn't work, he wouldn't go back for a redo on any of them. Within each one, there was a lesson that helped to shape the person he is today.

When I asked David if he had any final thoughts on success, he mentioned the movie, *The Greatest Showman.* He said he could really relate to the main character because he was a dreamer just like David. However, the character got caught up in his dreams at the expense of what was important to him. In the final scene of the movie, he's sitting at his daughter's ballet and the song playing in the background was *This Is The Greatest Show.*

No matter what success means to you, the meaningful relationships in your life are the "greatest show." Never lose sight of what's most important to you – the things money will never buy.

Jenny Butler
Patience

"Success is in the attempts."

Jenny Butler

W hen I asked Jenny what word she'd use to describe their journey so far, she told me that it would have to be patience. When you're the steady and stabilizing force behind the scenes, patience is most definitely a virtue.

Jenny loves being a stay-at-home mom and taking care of the couple's six kids. David recognizes that this is a full-time job and has always supported her in that role. Jenny is definitely David's number one fan, and they are the perfect complement to each other.

As David was constantly trying new things on his quest to find a career that would scratch his internal itch, Jenny maintained her steady it-will-all-work-out attitude throughout. She said she was never worried because she had complete confidence in David's multitude of eclectic skillsets.

Growing up, David was accustomed to a life of financial comfort and came to anticipate it. In fact, David shared with me that as a kid, if they wanted to play sports, there was never a question of whether he could get those new cleats or that new baseball bat. That kind of freedom – the freedom to say "yes" was the mark of success for him.

Jenny, on the other hand, didn't have a lot of money growing up but she always had a lot of fun and a very happy childhood. As David worked his way through many different jobs, she never had anxiety about his ability to provide for their family. She knew that whatever he did, he would make enough money to support the family. David put enough pressure on himself as the family provider.

The Journey

David and Jenny's time in Hawaii had a lasting impact on their lives. Besides, acquiring their family motto, they learned the fine art of relationship building. In the Islands, they were surrounded by people who didn't have a lot. Jenny believes that when you don't have a list of "things" or spend all of your time focused on how you're going to get more things, relationships can develop very quickly.

She explained that there are no schedules, and everything moves slower in the Islands. People there make you feel like you are their number one priority and nothing in the world is more important than listening and interacting with you. That's a unique and rare skill these days and one that people notice. No matter their socio-economic standing, all people want to be seen, heard and appreciated.

While Jenny built her listening skills in Hawaii, David mastered his time management skills. When David gets together with people, there is no schedule. He can just be with people until they're done and then he moves onto something else. Jenny admits that she still carves out blocks of time and sticks to her time budget.

David and Jenny's home has an open-door policy. When people come over, they are always welcomed with open arms. They both believe that our primary purpose on Earth is to love all of God's people regardless of race, religion, or political views. Jenny is proud of the standard that David sets for the kids in this area. Their family loves all people deeply.

One of the biggest challenges for Jenny so far has been watching David's relentless search for meaning in his career. She just wanted him to be doing something that he loves. David says that she has never even hinted that he shouldn't try something because of cost and then she makes room for him to try. It's one of the things he loves about her.

To Jenny, success on this journey is not a destination but rather, it is measured in the attempts. She believes that if you're moving in a direction that puts you in a better place mentally, emotionally, or spiritually - that is success. It's important to find peace and be comfortable in all aspects of life.

Jenny has noticed a slight shift in the dynamics with some of her friends and she admits that it has been a little bit of a challenge for her. For a long time, they lived paycheck to paycheck. She said for her, in some respects, it was easier to talk to people before they became successful.

She said that before, when she was talking to her friends, whose spouses were teachers, they'd all have fun commiserating together and joking about not having money. Now things are different for Jenny.

She's grateful that they are making more money but sometimes in social situations, she still talks as though she can't afford things and then feels like she's not being entirely truthful. She still wants to communicate with people on their level and be real. David and Jenny have made some good financial decisions and she'd like to be able to share that with some of her friends, but many are not in the same position, and she feels awkward.

Lessons From Mom

When I asked Jenny about the lessons she'd like to pass onto her kids about success, she said that she'd like them to remember to do something every day that is meaningful to their own person. Do something every day that makes you feel like you have purpose and makes you feel good.

She'd like her kids to keep trying and be willing to take risks when something is important to them. She wants them to have the courage to follow their dreams even when they may not be popular with those around them.

Their oldest son will be graduating from high school soon. He has a strong entrepreneurial spirit and does not want to go to college. He wants to start a business and she believes he will be successful.

Jenny admits she had to get used to the idea. One of her grandfathers was the head of Utah Valley University for years and the other was an English professor. Education in her family was just what you did, and it was expected of you. You graduated from high school and then went to college.

Jenny found the whole idea shocking until she realized that he was passionate about it. She respects her son for wanting to take a different route on his journey.

She also hopes to instill the concept of service to others in her kids. It forces you to look beyond yourself and your own needs. It's a strong component in building relationships and you can't help but feel good when you do it.

Hindsight

If she could go back, Jenny wouldn't change a thing. She loves David's spontaneity and his quest to always find something new and exciting to try. It's been quite an adventure so far. She is his rock, and she wouldn't have it any other way.

Lessons Learned From David And Jenny

D avid and Jenny have each played a vital role in their journey through to success. Their partnership thrives on mutual admiration and support and the path they've chosen together is one of patience and meaningful connections. This couple could have come no other way.

Jenny finds immense joy and fulfillment in her role as a stay-at-home mom, dedicating herself to the care of their six children. David recognizes the magnitude of her contribution and dedication to their home and family. He remains Jenny's number one fan, while she is his rock and a constant source of stability and encouragement.

Although no path to success is exactly linear, for most entrepreneurs, a singular career direction typically emerges fairly early. What strikes me about this couple is their unwavering confidence in David's drive and determination to excel at providing for their family, which allows him the freedom to keep his brilliant and inquisitive mind engaged and trying new endeavors.

While David embarks on his evolving search for a career that is both fulfilling and satisfies his creative itch, Jenny remains steadfast in her patient and optimistic perspective. She maintains complete confidence in David's eclectic skill set – never worrying or doubting his abilities to do whatever he sets his mind to.

Growing up with divergent financial backgrounds, David and Jenny bring their own unique perspectives to their success journey. David, accustomed to a life of financial comfort, equates success to his freedom to say "yes" to exploring his interests and trying new things.

In contrast, Jenny's was a childhood characterized by modest means, yet filled with happiness and cherished memories. She understands David's drive and determination and has complete faith in his ability to always support their family. David, in turn, places immense pressure on himself to excel in his role as the provider while still stretching toward his dreams.

Their transformative experiences in Hawaii had a profound influence on how they approach life, their priorities and who they are today. In the land of Aloha, they learned the fine art of building deep and meaningful relationships from a culture that has relationship-building imprinted in their very DNA.

Surrounded by individuals who valued personal relationships over "things," they quickly realized that by focusing less on acquiring material possessions, relationships flourished swiftly and organically. The slower pace of life in the islands magnified the importance of prioritizing people and fostering deep connections through active listening and genuine interactions. Both David and Jenny recognize the universal desire for acknowledgment and appreciation, regardless of socioeconomic standing.

As I listened to David and Jenny talk about relationships and patience, three central themes to their personal success journey became clear. The first is that they believe that strong relationships are fundamental to achieving long-term success in business, and in life.

They challenge the notion that technical expertise and strategic acumen alone are sufficient. Their business success highlights the power of building genuine connections with employees, customers, partners, stakeholders, friends, and family members. By nurturing these relationships, organizations (including families) can enhance productivity, foster innovation, and cultivate unbreakable loyalty and love.

Another thing that really struck me about this couple is their emphasis on the pivotal role that trust, and effective communication plays in building and maintaining the relationships in their lives. Trust is essential for creating an environment where collaboration, transparency, and teamwork thrive. Their authenticity, reliability and empathy are the tools they use for establishing trust in business and their family. They have become masters at open and transparent communication when resolving conflicts, aligning goals, and nurturing healthy relationships within their organizations and family.

Finally, they use every opportunity to encourage leaders and parents in their community to prioritize relationship-building by investing the time, energy and effort required to create and maintain meaningful connections. By consistently investing in relationships, the Butlers believe that you can foster loyalty, collaboration, and mutual success among everyone you interact with.

David and Jenny do not engage in deep meaningful relationships because of any business by-product they can create. They do it because they genuinely believe that people matter the most and by helping others become successful, they can't help but become successful in their own lives. It's this authenticity and sincerity that is the true magic in any relationship. This is the Spirit of Aloha that runs through their veins.

Aloha is a Hawaiian word that carries multiple meanings, such as love, compassion, peace, and harmony. The Spirit of Aloha encompasses a way of life and an attitude towards others that is characterized by kindness, respect, and a genuine care for the well-being of others.

The Spirit of Aloha is a cultural concept deeply rooted in Hawaiian traditions and values.

It goes beyond mere politeness or surface-level interactions. It is a way of being that emphasizes empathy, understanding, and a deep appreciation for the interconnectedness of all things. It is a guiding principle that encourages individuals to live with integrity, kindness, and a genuine concern for the well-being of others.

David and Jenny Butler *are* the Spirit of Aloha.

Chapter 10

Reflecting on Life's Journeys: The Fabric of Our Being

As we weave through the rich tapestry of David and Jenny Butler's life stories, we're encouraged to not merely witness their unique journey but rather, to explore the intricate patterns of our own lives. Their narrative is a vivid reminder of the diverse threads that create our existence: the dreams that propel us forward, the relationships that define us, and the values that underpin our every action.

As you stand at the intersection of their world and yours, take this time to reflect on how some of their experiences may resonate in your personal voyage. Jot down your thoughts, your realizations, and the actions they inspire. It is in these quiet moments of introspection that we often discover the most profound truths about ourselves.

Let the following questions be the loom on which you may begin to weave the next segment of your life's unique design.

1. **Dreams and Creativity:**
   - How have the dreams of my childhood shaped the person I am today?
   - What creative passions have I pursued or put aside?
2. **Influence of Parental Roles:**
   - In what ways have my parents' careers and lifestyle choices influenced my views on work, relaxation, and success?
3. **Spiritual Diversity and Openness:**
   - How has exposure to different beliefs and cultures affected my spiritual perspective?

- Do I actively seek understanding and common ground?

4. **Journeys and Partnerships:**
   - Reflecting on my significant relationships, how have chance encounters and decisions led to lasting bonds?
   - What role has spontaneity played in my life?

5. **Defining Success and Meaning:**
   - What does a successful life mean to me?
   - How do I balance the pursuit of material goals with the search for meaning and fulfillment?

As you ponder these questions, let them guide you to a deeper understanding of your own path and purpose. Allow the journey of David and Jenny Butler to illuminate your own, and may you find clarity and conviction in the steps you choose next.

Part 3

Karen and
Jeff Petersen

Chapter 11

Karen and Jeff Peterson Backstory

I f there was a single common denominator among everyone I've interviewed for this book, it would be that each couple I spoke to worked together closely as a team toward their family goals. Karen and Jeff are no different except that they have successfully turned the traditional concept of a team and team roles upside down.

Karen grew up in Virginia and attended Radford University before moving to North Carolina where she enrolled in the MBA program at the University of North Carolina. In the summer of 2000, Karen decided to visit an old friend in Utah. When she boarded that plane heading west, she couldn't possibly know just how life-changing the trip would be.

During her visit, she discovered The Church of Latter-Day Saints and became a sponge - anxious to learn everything she could about the church. Her friend also introduced her to a handsome guy who worked full-time at Home Depot. According to Karen, it was love at first sight in Electrical! She can still remember the shirt Jeff was wearing that day and although it would be another two years before they married, neither of them ever dated anyone else again.

When she returned home to North Carolina, Karen continued to study everything she could about the Church and when she was ready, it would be Jeff who baptized her. Karen knew where she belonged. She made her permanent move out to Utah and enrolled full-time in the BYU Marriott MBA marketing program.

As Karen worked through graduate school, Jeff continued to work at Home Depot and decided to start his own flooring business on the side. The couple married and Karen officially began her career in marketing, while Jeff focused on building his new company into a thriving one.

Karen worked as brand manager for two years and it wasn't long before the couple was expecting their first child. In fact, Karen was nine months pregnant when she made her first significant career move to Ancestry. She'd call the company home for the next 13 years.

It was a busy time for the Petersons. One thing you discover about Jeff almost instantly is he is an extremely hard worker – very service-oriented and thoughtful to everyone around him. His business grew quickly and soon, he supported several employees along with a solid reputation for dependability and quality work.

Meanwhile, Karen was busy moving up the ranks at Ancestry. She never pushed any particular career path or set her sights on specific title promotions. She simply focused on doing a good job and took advantage of every opportunity that was presented to her. During her tenure at Ancestry, she was promoted from senior manager to director, to senior director, to vice-president, to senior vice-president and eventually to Chief Marketing Officer.

As busy as they both were with their individual careers, family was always their top priority. Karen recalls as a child, never going to a babysitter, even though her mother worked as a highly respected pharmacist. Having a deep desire to follow her mother's example, the couple agreed from the time their first child was born that they would each stay home one day a week and Karen pioneered working remotely and was able to work from home on a regular basis.

Their system was hectic, but it worked – until 2008 when their second child was born. Gavin was born with Spina Bifida, a condition where the neural tube in the spine doesn't close all the way. He would have his first surgery within 24 hours of his birth and over that first year, he would endure 12 CAT scans and two surgeries.

According to Jeff, those first two days at the hospital would change the course of their lives forever. He knew having good medical insurance would be a must and because he was self-employed, he didn't have medical insurance at all except through Karen's job at Ancestry.

That whole first year they discussed their options. Should Jeff focus on growing his business or should he go back to school? They even talked about making less money so they could qualify for assistance but that just didn't feel right to them. It was a stressful time as they desperately tried to figure out what course of action would be the best for their family.

At a year old, Gavin was gradually becoming more mobile. One day Karen arrived at the office to discover that management had a proposition for her. Ancestry wanted her to open an office in Toronto. Sure, that Jeff would say no, she called him anyway and was shocked when he said that he'd consider it!

The decision would mean dramatic changes in both their lives. Jeff would have to close his business and would not be able to get a work visa in Canada. It meant he would have to transition from entrepreneur to full-time Mr. Mom. It also meant that Karen would bear the immense pressure of becoming the sole breadwinner for her family – and do so in a different country.

They discussed if from every possible angle before making their decision. They were strong in their faith, and they believed in each other – so Karen and Jeff decided to go for it!

Looking back on it now, Jeff says the timing couldn't have been more perfect. Remember, it was the beginning of 2008, and construction was starting to wind down. Before the year was over, the bottom would completely drop out of the construction business.

Had he continued working, and Karen quit her job to take care of Gavin, not only would they not have had medical insurance but according to Jeff, the family would have ended up very, very poor.

I'm still in awe when I think about the monumental decision Karen and Jeff made together. Not many couples could have undergone such a dramatic role reversal – and done it so successfully.

Jeff went from being a successful business owner working hard and hanging out with friends, to trapped in a house with two kids, ages three and one, in a different country and not knowing another soul. Karen went from sharing financial responsibility for her growing family to working from morning until night, six days a week, knowing that her family's financial well-being rested solely on her shoulders.

Karen laughs that even with the abrupt reversal in their roles, they still had one thing in common. Jeff was usually the only man at the PTA, and she was usually the only woman in the boardroom.

The Church was an important constant for them during this transitional time. It gave them structure and discipline when life seemed even crazier and more chaotic than usual. It was the place they went to meet people who shared their values. They usually saw the same people every week and they were able to make friends fairly quickly.

Working together, the Petersons spent three successful years in Toronto. It was a time of tremendous growth and learning for every member of the family. When Karen discovered that she was pregnant again, the couple decided that it would be best for the family to return to the United States. Gavin's birth had been physically and emotionally draining on everyone and they wanted to be close to the doctors they knew and back with close friends.

Karen wasn't sure what her return to the United States would mean for her career at Ancestry, but they had always been extremely supportive of her in the past. Even though the company had grown significantly, she was sure that they would remain supportive of her – and she was right.

In less than a year, she was promoted to Marketing Vice-President. One Friday, Karen was asked to serve as interim Chief Marketing Officer and had to make a decision by Sunday. Once again, Karen and Jeff decided together that she would go for it.

It was the best of times. It was the worst of times. It was a very exciting but stressful time for Karen. She was traveling more than she ever had before – every other week at a minimum and often, it turned out to be every week. This took her away from the family far more than she wanted or ever dreamed she would be.

Karen recalls that when she first started her heavy travel schedule, the kids would cry and beg her not to leave which as a mother, was heartbreaking. As time went on, the kids acclimated as kids do. She said it got to a point where they would barely look up or say good-bye when she was leaving and that was even more heartbreaking.

Eventually, her schedule only allowed her four to five hours of sleep per night. When it started to affect her health, the couple decided it was time for her to leave even though she loved the job. Karen says it was the right decision for her family and when she finally left, she felt good about it.

Ancestry had grown into a multi-billion-dollar company over Karen's 13 years with them. She was proud of the work she'd done and how she'd grown personally, but she was ready for a new challenge. In 2018, she settled into a new position as CMO for

BrainStorm, an up-and-coming software company, where she stayed for two years.

In 2020, she took a new CMO position at Lendio. She loves the work she's doing there connecting small business owners with lender capital around the country. Her work took on a new sense of urgency with entrepreneurs as the Covid pandemic spread.

After making her mark at Lendio and guiding small business owners through the uncertain and tumultuous times that accompanied the pandemic, Karen sought to leverage her vast marketing acumen in an industry close to her heart. In 2022, she embraced the role of Chief Marketing Officer at Chatbooks, a company revolutionizing the way families preserve their memories.

At Chatbooks, Karen's innovative strategies and deep understanding of storytelling have been instrumental in shaping the brand's narrative. Her leadership is enhancing the emotional connection between Chatbooks and its growing customer base. As of now, Karen continues to drive the company's marketing efforts, ensuring that each family's story is beautifully told and cherished through Chatbooks' products.

Karen and Jeff are truly a power couple and bring new meaning to conventional roles in a marriage. They both chose to move out of their comfort zone for the good of their family. In the next two chapters, they will share the lessons that their new roles and the challenges that came with them have taught them about   success.

Chapter 12

Karen Peterson
Teamwork

"The paycheck just happens to come in my name, but we do it together and we both work equally hard."

Karen Peterson

Karen Peterson is recognized and admired throughout the business world for her marketing genius and innovation. However, there's another skill for which she's widely known and in interviews, frequently finds herself fielding questions on. That is her ability to build and lead high-performing, successful teams wherever she is. It's not surprising that Karen and Jeff were able to do the same in their marriage.

According to Karen, there are several non-negotiable components that go into creating a powerful team. First, it's essential that everyone on a team be clear on the common goal and what specifically they're working to accomplish. In the case of Karen and Jeff, the common goal has always been family. This was true even before they had children, and they were each pursuing their separate careers. One + one has always equaled three with this couple.

It's also important that the right culture and attitude be present if a team is to be successful. Karen has seen it all and explained that sometimes, you may have a person on the team who is very good at their job but is also very difficult to work with. On the flip side, you may have a team member who is wonderful to work with but isn't particularly outstanding at what they do. Power teams bring the best of both worlds to the table.

Karen will be the first to tell you that Jeff is the hardest worker she has ever met — at whatever he chooses to pursue. His endless energy and extreme focus combined with his service mindset is a big part of why their team works. She's quick to point out that if it wasn't for the person that Jeff is, there would be zero chance that the couple be where they are today. He is humble and confident and if that wasn't the case, she firmly believes that their relationship could have turned into an unhealthy and unproductive competition.

Instead, they both place extreme value on the role each plays on their team. They support each other unconditionally and they strive to help each other become the very best that they can be. Karen describes Jeff as a sensitive guy but not one to shy away from delivering tough love when necessary. He often pushes her before she's ready, she adds, and he never allows her to wallow in depression or upset.

Karen shared that over the years, she's had all kinds of personalities in her personal network. Some she says, make you feel better, make you laugh, and you know are always on your side. However, it's the people that push you that she has grown to appreciate the most. Jeff, more than anyone else, is and has always been that person for Karen.

Baby Steps To Their Success

When I asked Karen what she felt were some key steppingstones to their success, she prefaced her comments by saying that in most cases, it comes down to the basics – in church, in business and in life. It's about developing those consistent little habits that are often the hardest yet can make the biggest difference when you need it the most.

One of the most important is gratitude. Author, Amy Rees Anderson said, "A person who feels appreciated will always do more than expected." Karen has practiced this in business and at home. She looks for reasons to be grateful and to send little notes of appreciation whenever possible – especially to Jeff. She communicates to him on a consistent basis just how vital his role is and how important his work is to the family and to her.

Jeff's passion is dirt bikes and it's much more than a hobby to him. It's his gym – his exercise – his release. It's a time for him to be alone with his thoughts out in nature and away from his work responsibilities at home. Karen recognizes how important it is to him but has always viewed it as a dangerous sport. Even though it's taken awhile for her to fully accept and admittedly, she will probably always worry, she understands that it is vital for him to have that personal time to do what he loves. Her willingness to support him in his passion, Karen considers this a definite baby step in their success as a team.

A habit that has always been sacred to them from the very beginning is family dinners. If Karen is in town, they find a way to have dinner together as a family. It's important to both Karen and Jeff and it's a tradition they want to pass along to their children. Karen envisions the family always congregating around the dinner table to laugh and share stories – even when the kids are grown.

Another important baby step that Karen practices consistently is calling Jeff every night on her way home. Even if she has to make another call, she will still take the time to talk to him even if it's briefly. Karen usually works until 6:00 or 7:00 every night. Jeff runs a tight ship at home and the kids are typically in bed by 8:30. Those phone calls from the car give them a chance to download their day so that Karen has more time to spend with the kids when she gets home.

This is also a way for Jeff to stay involved and in a better position to support Karen. He knows everything that goes on at the office, the players, the dynamics – everything. He's not only a great sounding board for her, but he has tremendous insight into people. According to Karen, he has a way of diffusing the drama and emotion out of a situation, helping her to make the best decisions possible.

Defining Success

Karen has always loved school and the whole structure that school offers. You know where you're supposed to be at what time. You know what you have to do specifically to be successful. There's a clear and definite measurement system and built-in feedback loop that makes defining success relatively easy.

She found out very quickly that in the business world, success isn't nearly as clear. Karen was forced to acclimate to a system with no set scores nor a consistent feedback mechanism for determining where exactly you were on the success scale. In some instances, you received no feedback which made it nearly impossible to know what should be changed.

Karen prefers to have success milestones quantifiable and measurable. She was forced to develop her own measures of success relatively quickly. A primary method Karen uses for defining success is her ability to create value for the company. Are her efforts raising company revenue and/or enhancing the customer experience? Karen is a firm believer that the hierarchy in business should always be: customer – company – team – individual.

She also measures success by the degree to which she empowers people. Karen explains that everyone wants to win and loves to win. When she builds a team that is seeing success and working well together, it increases job happiness which in turn fuels optimism. She defines optimism as the ability to always find a path forward. It may not be the path you wanted or expected but Karen believes that there are always multiple right answers and her ability to identify these and move forward is one of her strengths.

To Karen, optimism is a very important component of success. She has witnessed firsthand that negativity tends to spread much faster than positivity. When facing a negative situation in business or in life, it's important that you look for what you can control and focus on that.

You don't have to know all the answers but often, success is measured in how adaptive of a learner you can be. Humility plays a big part in this. You have to be open enough to be willing to listen to other people and not close yourself off – thinking your way is the only way.

When Karen was working as the CMO for Lendio, she fell in love with their tagline – humble and hungry. To Karen, the two together are powerful and often define exactly what it takes to become successful.

The Price of Success

Karen always thought she'd follow in her mother's successful footsteps. Although her mother was a professional woman working as a pharmacist, she'd worked on and off as needed. She just thought it was a given and all moms did that. However, that was not the case for Karen.

She always wanted to be that mom that took one or two years off to be with her new babies. The most she ever got for maternity leave was 12 weeks and it felt wrong to Karen. She spent years and years feeling that it wasn't supposed to be that way – questioning her success as a mother.

In Karen's mind, lost time with her children was the price she paid for her success. It took a long time for her to wrap her mind around that and to feel like everything fit into place. She had to change her perspective and accept that there were probably very good reasons why things worked out the way they did for the good of her family – reasons she might never understand.

Some moments are still hard for her, and she wished could have been different, but she and Jeff knew what they were getting into. They always made decisions together and those decisions were always made with the good of the family as their top priority. It took awhile, but she is at peace with it now.

Karen believes that the wisdom gained from the sacrifices she made has molded her into a better team leader. She's the first one to tell her employees to go on that field trip and don't miss that school function. She's quick to remind them that no one ever wins a prize for spending all night on the phone or working through a family vacation. Her perspective not only endears her to her employees, but it helps her to empower the people who work with her.

Lessons Learned

It wasn't surprising that when I asked Karen about the lessons she learned on her journey, she spoke of happiness. Her words of wisdom certainly rang true to me. She said that all too often, we tend to think that we will be happy when we become successful. However, to Karen the opposite is true.

When you find happiness first, it makes success – in whatever way you choose to define it – not only easier to achieve but sweeter when you reach it. She added that finding happiness is a journey in itself.

Karen shared with me that it's important that you spend time getting to know who you really are and what you value. Understand why you do what you do and how that aligns with your values. Only then can you really begin to understand where your joy and happiness lie and how it all fits together. It's then that you begin to gain peace and a positive perspective in all you do and to Karen, that is the true meaning of success.

Chapter 13

Jeff Peterson
Adaptability

"Don't stray from the basic fundamentals like communication and trust – everything else you can adapt to."

Jeff Peterson

A ccording to a recent Today Show survey, "51% of dads said they would quit working and stay home with kids if they could afford it. 78 % of dads who do stay at home said that that society underestimates them."[2]

Underestimating Jeff would be a big mistake. He's not your ordinary guy. He's a man's man. He's confident, loves dirt bikes, works hard every day and when something needs to be done, he's the first one to step up to do it and do it well. He also likes a clean house, takes care of four kids and runs a tight ship at home.

Providing for the family financially has traditionally been the man's role. With Karen and Jeff, it is truly a 50/50 team effort. They've always shared a deep desire to provide for their family in the best way possible and if that meant bucking gender role trends, then so be it.

The original plan when they got married was that Karen would be the stay-at-home mom. They never aspired to be the kind of parents who spent all day just working to get stuff. They wanted to be a big part of their children's lives and didn't want them going to day care every day. It was important to them both that one parent could be home and there for their kids when they were growing up.

---

[2] "Today: Stay-at-Home Dads On The Rise & Overcoming the "Mr. Mom" Stigma," Recapo, accessed October 18, 2022, https://www.recapo.com/today-show/today-show-advice/today-stay-home-dads-rise-overcoming-mr-mom-stigma/.

When Gavin was born with Spina Bifida, it took less than 24 hours for the couple to realize that their life plans were about to radically change. Their number one priority instantly became ensuring that he would have access to the best medical care possible and he would have the extra care he needed at home to grow and flourish.

Karen had just started a dream job with great benefits at Ancestry and although Jeff's business was booming, as a self-employed entrepreneur, he didn't have the medical benefits their son would need. They analyzed all possible options. Ancestry was growing rapidly, and they believed Karen's career could advance with it.

They made their decision together and although the plan had changed, their commitment to family had not. It was decided that Jeff would stay at home and provide for the kids there and Karen would pursue her career and provide for their family financially.

Lessons In Adapting

One of the first questions I asked Jeff when we sat down to talk regarded the words he'd use to describe his journey. Without hesitation, he responded "adapting." Obviously, the role reversal in providing for their family required strong adaptation skills but as Jeff pointed out, they were no strangers to the concept of adapting. They'd been doing it from the beginning.

When they first met, Karen lived in North Carolina and Jeff lived in Utah. Karen's move to Utah carried a lot of uncertainty with it and she had to adapt to new surroundings, a new home, a new school, and a new love in her life.

When Jeff decided to leave Home Depot and work full-time at his new flooring business, he had a crash course in adapting. Transitioning from the security of a regular paycheck to the uncertainty of running a new business is always a big change. He had to learn how to consistently get new customers and manage employees effectively.

Karen and Jeff had to learn to adapt together when Gavin was born. In addition to having to grow into their new roles as parents and providers, they had to adjust to their own physical and emotional challenges as well as Gavin's.

Moving to Canada provided another lesson in adapting for the couple. They were in a strange country where they didn't know anyone. There was a new home, new schools, new schedules, a new church congregation and new job to get used to.

Even when they returned home and Karen was offered the CMO job at Ancestry, the entire family had to adapt to her new travel schedule. Although it wasn't easy on the kids, it required patience and extraordinary commitment on the part of Karen and Jeff.

If there's a gene for the ability to successfully adapt, Karen and Jeff must both have it. Any one of these dramatic changes in circumstances would have taken a serious toll on most couples - but not this one. Karen and Jeff seem to have the uncanny ability to navigate through change almost effortlessly with grace and poise.

The Peterson Secret Sauce

It's my personal opinion that very few couples could have achieved the level of success that Jeff and Karen have in the way that they have. They are truly a unique and special couple. So how do they do it?

When I asked Jeff that question, he had some strong opinions on the subject. He believes that open, honest communication and collaboration with your partner is essential to staying focused on what's most important to you both.

Communicating your needs to each other is not only healthy but it's key to knowing how to best help each other. According to Jeff, bottling your feelings up inside rarely turns out well. He chuckled when he added that expressing them doesn't always work out well either. Evidently, he can be brutally honest about his feelings, but he still believes it's always better to get everything out in the open and talk about it.

It takes guesswork out of the equation and fosters trust. It's where true collaboration begins. When everything is out in the open, it's much easier to identify and analyze different options before deciding together on the best course of action.

Jeff also believes that maintaining and refusing to compromise on their morals and standards has been a critical component in their success. Once you allow a change in the fundamentals of who you are and what's important to you, everything changes and often implodes.

The core principles that Karen and Jeff share are non-negotiable to them and that can be something as simple as trust. Jeff uses the example of Karen's traveling and time away. The people she works with everyday are 90% men and that can be even higher when she travels. Meanwhile back at home, Jeff spends time scheduling playdates with other Moms every day. If you were to remove or compromise the basics like trust and communication, it would throw their whole life together out of balance. The couple feels very fortunate that their values and standards align so well.

Both Karen and Jeff are very hard workers, and he believes that their strong work ethic has also played a role in their success. They both know that the other is working just as hard as they are every day.

Jeff can't remember a time when he didn't want to work hard. When he was eight years old, his family lived in Denver and his older brother had a paper route. He wanted one too but was too young, so his parents signed up for a paper route that was his responsibility. He said he rode his bike in the snow delivering newspapers at 5:30 in the morning and the snow had to be pretty deep for his father to drive him.

He grew up in a "no excuses" household and it's something he wants to pass along to his kids. Jeff recalls when Gavin was learning to walk with a walker, he would grow frustrated and want to give up, but Jeff wouldn't allow it. Instead, he drew squares in chalk in the driveway to guide him. Gavin would complain but he learned to walk.

Jeff tries to push his kids and especially Gavin. He thinks that in many ways, women are better and more nurturing in his role. Sometimes he admits that Karen has to remind him to spoil the kids a little and that it can't be just about cleaning and work. On occasion, she'll gently suggest that he take them to the park or out for a treat. Again, it's that open and honest communication that makes their world work.

Defining Success

As with most people, Jeff's definition of success has changed and evolved over the years. At different points in his life, success was financially driven. When they were first married, he related success to being in a position to buy a house and later, building his business. Once Karen graduated, success became more about starting and supporting a family. When Gavin was born, it evolved into providing the very best in medical care for their son.

With success, many times it's all related to money –
sometimes out of fear. However, when all your
motivation is thrown behind the money aspect of
success, it's sometimes easy to lose sight of the desire
you had for that money. Jeff maintains balance in how
he views success because he wants to avoid the risk of
one day waking up and realizing he's living a life filled
with "stuff" he never really wanted.

These days, Jeff views success as being content and
happy – dirt bikes and Karen (not necessarily in that
order). Sometimes to him, it can be as simple as the kids
listening or having an aha moment. More than anything,
he feels it's about keeping life balanced – something
they both work very hard to do for themselves and their
family.

Chapter 14

Lessons Learned From Karen and Jeff

n the tapestry of life and business, few threads are as intricately woven as the journey of Karen and Jeff Peterson. Their story – a mosaic of ambition, faith, adaptability, and partnership, serves as an exemplary testament to the power of collaboration in both personal and professional realms.

The Petersons are not just a "power couple" in the traditional sense. Rather, they redefine what power means within a partnership and marriage. Their story challenges societal expectations and proves that roles within a marriage can be fluid and adaptable and still work to satisfy the evolving needs of the family.

What stands out the most to me is their extraordinary resilience – Karen, with her unyielding dedication to her work and family, and Jeff, with his unwavering commitment to adapt and provide for his family in whatever way is needed. Their adaptability, through the unpredictable twists and turns of life, showcases the strength of their bond. However, it's not just adaptability that makes their story compelling. It's their unity of purpose, their shared vision, their unwavering faith, and their endless commitment to their family's well-being that is so remarkable.

For the business owners and their spouses reading this, the Petersons' story should serve as a guide. It emphasizes that the journey to success is not linear. It's typically riddled with decisions guaranteed to remove you from your comfort zone. Although intimidating, it's these decisions that often lead to unanticipated blessings and opportunities. For Jeff, the unexpected role reversal led him to cherish fatherhood from a totally unique vantage point he would have never experienced otherwise. For Karen, her corporate trajectory allowed her to influence and mentor many people while providing for her family in a significant way.

The couple's faith, evident in their every decision, acts as their North Star, guiding them through challenges and uncertainties. To the Petersens, the Church is far more than just a place of worship. To them, it serves as a sanctuary of support and community. A key takeaway from Karen and Jeff is to find that anchor that keeps your relationship grounded and nurture it – whether it's faith, shared goals, or mutual passions.

Another profound lesson from the Petersons' journey lies in recognizing the importance of communication and understanding in a relationship. Whether it's Karen acknowledging Jeff's need for his dirt-biking escapades or Jeff supporting Karen's career choices, their mutual respect and understanding for each other's needs is palpable. Their mantra of open communication, trust, and the unwillingness to compromise on core values forms the very foundation of their relationship.

Their narrative also underscores the meaning of gratitude. Their constant appreciation for each other, celebrating small victories, and acknowledging the value each brings to the table keeps their bond strong and unwavering. In a world that often pushes individual achievements, their story is a refreshing reminder of the joy and power of collaborative success.

For business owners and spouses alike, the Petersons' story is not just about achieving success but about redefining it. It's about understanding that success is not just measured by societal standards or financial achievements but by personal contentment, happiness, and the positive impact one makes in the lives of others.

In conclusion, Karen and Jeff Peterson's journey offers a multi-faceted lesson: a lesson in resilience, partnership, faith, and in the unyielding pursuit of happiness and contentment. Their story encourages every reader to embrace change, to communicate openly, and most importantly – to prioritize family and personal well-being over societal norms.

In a world that often glorifies individual achievements, the Petersons stand out as a testament to the fact that the journey is richer, more meaningful, and infinitely more rewarding when undertaken hand-in-hand. Theirs is a narrative of hope, love, and of the beauty of shared dreams. It's a story that reminds us that together, we can face any challenge, scale any height, and redefine the paradigms of success.

Chapter 15

Reflecting on Life's Journeys: Embracing Change and Unity

As we close the page on Karen and Jeff Peterson's story, we encounter a narrative rich with change, commitment, and collective strength. Their journey illuminates the power of unity in marriage, the fluidity of roles, and the resilience required to navigate life's unexpected paths.

I encourage you to take a moment now to pause and reflect upon your own journey. What challenges have you faced, and how have you adapted? How do you define success and fulfillment within the framework of your relationships and personal aspirations?

Take some time to consider these questions. Write down your thoughts, the parallels you draw between the Petersons' experiences and your own and consider any actions that come to mind. These reflections can become a blueprint for the future chapters in your own life, guiding you towards a narrative that embraces change with grace, and unity with conviction.

1. **Examining Role Flexibility:**
   - How flexible am I in my roles within my personal and professional life?
   - What can I learn from Karen and Jeff's ability to adapt to new situations and challenges?
2. **Considering the Impact of Faith and Community:**
   - What role does faith or community play in my life?
   - How does it support me through my own transitions and decisions?
3. **Understanding Partnership in Decision Making:**

- How do I collaborate with my partner or support system when faced with life-altering decisions?
- What can be improved in our communication and decision-making processes?

4. **Reflecting on Work and Family Balance:**
   - How do I balance the demands of my career with the needs of my family?
   - What strategies can I employ to ensure that neither is neglected?

5. **Defining Personal Success:**
   - What is my definition of success?
   - How does it align with my values, happiness, and the well-being of my family?

As you delve into these questions, let the resilience and unity of Karen and Jeff's story inspire you to navigate your own life with similar courage and togetherness.

Part 4

Jared and
Cherise Rodman

Chapter 16

Jared and Cherise Rodman Backstory

Michael J. Fox once said, "Family is not an important thing. It is everything." Jared and Cherise Rodman personify this concept every single day. It was Jared's desire to help his brother that started him down his path to success, and having a happy, healthy family has always been the standard by which the couple defines and measures their success.

A strong work ethic is part of Jared's DNA. However, to hear him tell it - he's just incredibly lucky. While that may be true, it was his consistent effort and patience that kept him going while waiting for his lucky streak to kick in.

Jared was a Physics major and working in sales when he and Cherise were married in 2008. At that time, he thought that patent law might be his calling. In the fall of that year, despite a new marriage, a challenging sales job and a full school schedule - in Physics no less, Jared decided to help his brother by working as an outbound sales rep in Brandon's new company, Recall Solutions. Family first, right?

Jared and Brandon's mom was a dental hygienist, and they were quite familiar with the issues dental practices faced in scheduling patients for regular cleanings. The idea was - Recall Solutions would acquire lists of overdue patients from local dentists and rather than the dental support staff trying to reach patients afterhours, the company would call to get the patients scheduled.

They started in the attic above Brandon's garage and were signing up new dental practices every month. Although the company was growing rapidly, they felt they still weren't reaching enough of the patients they were trying to schedule. In an effort to improve their numbers, they decided to add a texting feature, and the idea paid off. Not only were they able to reach more patients but it became obvious relatively quickly that most people preferred to schedule via text at their own convenience.

Over the next couple of years, Jared continued his balancing act as his time commitment to the company continued to increase. In 2011, they decided to package everything from their scheduling services into a full-integrated software package that they could market to dental offices. They changed the name to Weave to better depict how all the necessary components were "weaved" together for maximum efficiency.

Jared's schedule was becoming unmaintainable. Although he'd quit his other sales job, he was still going to school full-time, managing the Weave call center and running payroll. His days were long with classes in the morning and working at Weave usually from 1:00-9:00 PM. He'd then rush home to tackle homework and try to fit some family time in where he could.

It didn't take long for Jared to realize he had to make a conscious decision about the future. In 2011, he decided to give up his law aspirations. He changed his major, became a co-founder in Weave and committed full-time to the company.

By 2013, because of the company's rapid growth, they were starting to run out of money. After exhausting all possible funding opportunities with venture capitalists and angel investors in Utah, they tried one more time with a company in California and to their surprise, they were accepted.

Weave was on a roll. From 2014-2020, they continued raising capital, scaling, and experiencing tremendous growth. The company now had a board of directors, and their valuation was set at nearly $1 Billion. Just when Brandon and Jared should have been on top of the world, the board shocked them with the news that they were replacing Brandon with a new CEO. They felt the company had outgrown Brandon and wanted a new CEO to take the company to the next level.

On November 11, 2021, the company that the brothers had built from nothing went public on the New York Stock Exchange. After all the blood, sweat and tears Brandon and Jared had put in over the previous 13 years, the board and new CEO chose not to extend an invitation to them to participate in the event at all. Instead, they celebrated quietly with their families.

The year that Weave went public was a tough one for Jared. He admits that things did not unfold the way he would have wanted or expected but he explains - that's just the way it happens sometimes in life. He knew he had to take the time to process his emotions about the situation.

Cherise acknowledges that this was a rough time, and it was hard watching him work through everything. However, she adds that through it all, he never neglected his family duties. During that time, she felt her emotions had to be put on the back burner. She tried to be a support for him and not let her own feelings get in the way of always being there to listen when he wanted to talk.

According to Jared, Cherise was instrumental in helping him work through things and arrive at the other side. Choosing to become an entrepreneur guarantees a roller-coaster ride. For Jared, in those moments when the roller-coaster hits the bottom, hearing an "I love you," or "It doesn't matter" from Cherise felt like a giant weight had been lifted from his shoulders.

Her love never waivers and knowing that, he admits, has been a key component in his success. He is quick to point out that nothing could have ever happened without the support of his wife.

When all of the events transpired at Weave, Jared said he was angry and he brooded - for awhile - but ultimately, it was up to him to look for the life lessons and be willing to learn from them. The decision he made in this experience, and he continues to make in his life, is to be grateful for the lessons life offers and use them to become a better person.

When Jared and Cherise got married, Cherise says they were very upfront about how they wanted their marriage to operate. They both wanted an equal partnership. They also understand that in a marriage, it's not always going to be 50/50. Sometimes one person may need to take a time out when going through a really hard time and that's okay. This is just one of the lessons they learned from their Weave experience.

From the very beginning, they knew they wanted to build a strong and stable team together. To do that, they both recognized the importance of good communication. Cherise admits that their marriage hasn't always been smooth sailing. When they felt like they weren't communicating well and started having more disagreements – they were committed to fixing it together, so they went to counseling and worked on it.

They both agree that the skills they've learned in counseling have taught them how to communicate better. Their communication skills, which they continually work to improve upon have been a key factor in their success.

Jared thinks everyone should go through the counseling experience whether they think they need it or not. He feels there are tremendous benefits to be gained - if you're committed to the process.

Cherise adds that having kids changes everything. As your family grows, you have to be able to grow with it. When challenges come up, constant communication and collective decision-making is essential. Their commitment to learning how to communicate with each other effectively has paid off – time and time again throughout their marriage.

Chapter 17

Jared Rodman
Family First

"I define success as the health and stability of our family. Family is a core value."

Jared Rodman

H ow we experience life is largely determined by the decisions and choices we make every day. This is why an individual's life experiences are as unique as their fingerprint - and so is their definition of success.

Jared has always had very definitive thoughts on what constitutes success but he's also a serious student of life. As such, he looks for the lessons that life offers him. As he continues to grow and evolve – so have his thoughts on the subject of success.

Prior to working with his brother at Weave, he defined success as more of a mindset – one characterized by stability, having a trade and a good job to back it up. For many, including Jared in the beginning, that meant following the traditional path of college and post-graduate work. However, he has never been one to accept or be satisfied with the status quo. Combine that trait with his loyalty and devotion to family and it's not surprising he ended up working with his brother and becoming a cofounder at Weave.

Looking back on his journey now, Jared admits that he probably didn't fully grasp the risk he was taking at the time, or the position he was putting Cherise in by ditching the traditional path to success for the entrepreneurial one. They had just gotten married and didn't have any heavy financial commitments. They weren't in debt apart from some school loans and because they didn't have any children yet, they had the flexibility he felt they needed to be able to take a risk.

Back then, Jared says he always knew he could change course if they needed to. Cherise was working at the time and from a financial standpoint, they were relatively free to take a chance on an opportunity. A lot of times, people view their decisions as a one-way door, but Jared looks at most decisions as more of a revolving door with the ability to move in and out and shift as need be.

However, if he were faced with taking those kinds of risks now with kids, he admits the decision would be infinitely more difficult. Without an income or even a significantly reduced one, it would take significantly more thought and planning – if feasible at all. Family first is not just a catchy phrase – it's the basis of every decision Jared makes. The criteria he measures every decision by? He has to believe the decision in the best interest of his entire family.

Jared believes that success is something that everyone must define for themselves. Even if someone's definition of success is the same or similar to yours, it doesn't mean you can replicate their success by following the same steps. Mentors are everywhere and Jared thinks that you can learn something from everyone. It's up to each individual to carve out their own path to their own definition of success, which is exactly what he did.

In many ways, he thinks success is almost a misnomer – like perfection. Success will always mean different things to different people. When it's all said and done, being true to yourself, what you stand for and what you truly want out of life is what really matters.

Jared prefers to define success from an integrity standpoint. This means always holding true to his core values regardless of what's happening in and around his life. This was evident as he navigated the Weave situation.

For Jared, his "Family First" core value is the primary objective behind everything he does. He shared that when he reflects back over the decisions he's made and why he made them, he can invariably trace them back to that one value and his desire to provide the very best for his family. The health and stability of his family is the true standard by which he measures his success.

Having integrity and making decisions that are consistent with who he's decided and chooses to be is always the first stage of success. Beyond that, the ability to contribute to another's progression and success is important to subsequent stages of success.

Biggest Challenges

When I asked Jared about the biggest challenges he's faced on his success journey, I was surprised by his answer. Without hesitation, he said – forgiveness – and learning to forgive himself more than anyone else.

He explained that we live in a world of expectations. The weight we carry from the expectations we hold – some spoken, some we feel and never speak of, and some we may be totally unaware of – causes a lot of unnecessary and often, painful stress.

Forgiveness is huge to Jared. He believes that when we're able to forgive ourselves for our shortcomings and realize that we're all just people who make mistakes - trying to do better and make a positive difference to those around us – it gives us more freedom to do what is ours to do.

Regarding the Weave situation and forgiveness within a business context, Jared wished only to speak at a high level due to non-disclosure agreements he has in place with the company. He approached the discussion more philosophically and said that we all have the ability to choose how we will respond and feel in any situation. Jared said he could get angry – which he admits he was for a brief period of time, or he could choose to look for the lesson and grow from it.

He added that his departure from the Weave team obviously wasn't his decision. It was something that was decided for him. After allowing himself some time to just be angry, he shifted his focus on all that he was grateful for during his time at Weave. He spent time and energy on processing what he'd learned and how he could use those lessons to become a better person and put himself in a better position going forward. Part of success, after all, is not letting the dark times define you.

Jared's Success Recipe

When I interviewed Jared and Cherise, a recurring theme in their marriage, in their family and a key contributing factor in their success has been their unwavering commitment to good communication. To the Rodmans, that means nurturing openness and a willingness to be vulnerable in expressing how they really feel to each other.

Jared believes a good marriage depends on it. He explained that even with all the positive aspects woven into a marriage, thinking it's going to be all dandelions and rainbows is a mistake. The communication skills you develop as a couple evolve and mature into the skills you will eventually use with your kids.

Developing and maintaining good mental health is important to everyone but to an entrepreneur, it can quickly move from important to critical. An entrepreneur's life is filled with the highest highs and the lowest lows. It can be highly erratic – often chaotic and Jared believes every entrepreneur has the potential to spiral down if they're not careful. Counseling and its benefits have been a staple in Jared's recipe for success.

And of course – Cherise is the essential ingredient that made his success recipe work. Without her unwavering love and support, Jared will be the first to tell you that none of it would have happened. He trusts and values her opinion on what's best for their family. They make all of their decisions together and neither would have it any other way.

When I asked Jared what he would do differently if he had to do it all over again, he shared that he wasn't sure he'd do anything differently. Part of good mental health is the ability to look back and be grateful for the experiences that made them who they are today. Jared chooses to appreciate lessons learned – even the painful ones because those tough lessons impact who he is and how he acts today.

Jared says that the only way he would consider doing things differently is if they could be who they are today with all the knowledge, experience and growth they gained along the way but without the pain. However, he recognizes that without those difficult lessons, he'd be a different person living a very different life.

Another important ingredient to Jared's success is his commitment to exercise. He says he learned how important it is very early on and every morning at 6:30 – you'll find him at the gym. Having a strong body helps him have a strong and clear mind. In fact, Jared said that his days are composed of the three key elements – exercise, family and work and he won't compromise on any of the three.

Success Lessons For The Kids

Jared's goals for his kids are simple. Above all, he wants his kids to be happy and not only know they are loved but to feel that they are loved.

He wants them to spend the time to define success on their own terms. From both a religious and world standpoint, often, if a parent is perceived as doing something successful, there's a certain expectation that the children should achieve something equal or greater than the parent. Jared feels that can put unbearable pressure on a child and he doesn't want that for his children.

He believes that you're always teaching your children something with every interaction you have with them. There are always intentional and unintentional consequences of how they act with their kids. Both Jared and Cherise are aware of this and setting a good example for them is another demonstration of their core value – family first.

Jared wants his children to simply know what makes them happy. Find their passion and pursue that. Know what success means to them and strive to live their own definition of success. Nothing more.

Chapter 18

Cherise Rodman
Love Yourself

"Loving yourself is kind of like on an airplane when they tell you to secure your mask first before helping others."

Cherise Rodman

No one gets out of this life unscathed. Everyone has battled that little voice inside at one time or another judging you - telling you that you're not good enough and planting those seeds of doubt.

Jared and Cherise are no different. When Jared referenced mental health as an important factor in their success, Cherise concurred.

For many years, therapy and counseling has had a somewhat of a negative stigma attached to it. No more – in fact, quite the contrary. Like many women with busy families, Cherise used to feel guilty when taking any time for herself. Now, there's no doubt in her mind that it was an essential step for her to be her best.

Cherise will tell you that she put it off longer than she should have - even though she knew it would help. Learning to love and forgive herself has at times been a challenging path for her. She did not grow up in an ideal family. Her mom had to wear the hats of both mom and dad -often, working three jobs just to support the family.

There was even a time when her mother had to go on church assistance for food. At one point, they almost lost their home. However, one thing Cherise learned from her mom was that no matter what life throws at you, your life, and the paths you take are ultimately in your hands.

She admits - healing can be scary. Often, she had to relive things she'd tried to forget. You're opening old wounds all over again, but she knew something was missing. These old wounds were the very ones that she felt had kept her from being 100% for herself, Jared and her family – so, she endured. She's so grateful that she did because in the process, she learned to love and forgive herself.

Jared was a strong support to her throughout and actually embraced the process. Not only have they learned to communicate better but they both agree that the therapy and counseling process has helped them to become more patient with each other and accept each other for exactly who they are with no expectations. This can be incredibly liberating to everyone involved and they are grateful for the process.

It also equipped them to better deal with Jared's departure from Weave. As you know that situation was traumatic for them both. In many ways, it was like losing part of their family.

The Dark Days

Several years ago, if you ever drove on the freeway in the tech corridor in Utah, chances are you noticed the Weave billboard proudly declaring, "People, not employees." Jared's brother, Brandon originally coined the term but one of Jared's jobs was to cultivate that culture within the company and it's one he really enjoyed.

Cherise describes what she called an "Oprah Moment" years ago at the Weave Christmas party. Jared was on the stage talking about the company's accomplishments for the year. He was giving out very cool Christmas presents to everyone, and she realized what a tremendous impact he was having on people's lives.

She realized their slogan, "People, not employees" was more than a slogan. Jared had built it into a way of life at the company. He made people feel like they mattered, and each one was important. Weave employees were happy and had a purpose they believed in.

When Brandon and Jared were let go, it was a shock to everyone. Cherise recalls that they wouldn't even let him say good-bye to employees. Suddenly, all those relationships were gone.

After they left, employees were still trying to reach out to him and wanting to talk to him. Cherise said she was so thankful that in those dark days, Jared got to see a glimpse of just how much he'd affected their lives.

Her advice to other spouses who may one day have to go through something similar is to be there to listen. They don't need advice. What they need more than anything is a sounding board to let them express their feelings with no judgement – just love.

During that time, any extras she could do for Jared – she did. One of the hardest things for Jared was he was used to being so busy all the time and all of a sudden, he wasn't. He was just there with his feelings.

Cherise admits that those dark days affected her as well. She felt sad for Jared, but she also had a lot of friendships she'd developed through Weave. These relationships had been an important component of their success, and it was hard for both Jared and Cherise to let them go.

They stayed in touch with some people – having them over for dinner. They made a point of inviting them to do different things and they were able to keep some of their relationships going.

Defining Success

Cherise says she still can't believe that this is her life. She has everything she ever wanted and dreamed of – a loving husband, a family, and kids she adores!

When I asked her how she defined success, she said being true to herself is when she feels the most successful. She added that whenever she feels like she's straying from her beliefs or doing things just to please other people, it diminishes her feelings of being successful.

She also monitors success based on how she feels her family is doing. Cherise's role in this partnership is to ensure that everyone is taken care of. She does all the planning, scheduling, logistics, carpooling and cooking. It's a role she loves and takes very seriously.

If the family is doing well, she feels like the kids are happy and her relationship with Jared is good then that is success to her. Cherise added that you can have all the money in the world but if things aren't going well at home or there's tension within the family, she doesn't feel successful as a wife and mom.

She's grateful that Jared is so supportive and is always there if she needs help with anything. She does homework with their oldest son. He helps out with baths and getting the kids to bed. They love it when Dad reads to them before bed.

He also mans the fort when Cherise takes her annual girls' trip every October. Interestingly enough, the girls' idea of fun is to go someplace in the country that has a reputation for being haunted. Over the years, they've visited some of the most haunted places in America.

Entrepreneurship is part of Jared's DNA. He's teamed up with his brother in their new venture, Previ. What the future holds for this couple, who's to say? One thing is for sure, they will work as a strong team in getting it done.

Chapter 19

Lessons Learned From Jared and Cherise

As we reach the end of our journey through the lives of this remarkable couple, we want to take a moment to reflect on the powerful lessons that they have shared with us. Their unwavering commitment to each other built on a foundation of self-love and choices serves as a shining example for anyone seeking to cultivate a successful and fulfilling relationship.

One of the most profound realizations we can gleam from their story is that one of our greatest gifts in life is the ability to choose. This couple's conscious decision to prioritize their relationships and invest in communication and choose family above all else has been a primary driving force behind their success.

This power of choice is something we all possess and embracing it can bring about transformative changes in our relationships and lives. Effective communication has played a critical role in this couple's journey – providing them with a powerful tool for navigating the complexities of life together.

Their willingness to listen, learn, and grow together has deepened their connection and fostered a sense of trust and mutual respect. By cultivating open and honest communication, we can create a stronger and more resilient relationship – one that can stand the test of time.

This couple's emphasis on putting family first demonstrates the value of nurturing our most precious bonds. By focusing on the needs of loved ones and prioritizing togetherness, they've created a support system that's carried them through some of their most challenging moments.

Choosing family first is not only an act of love – it's also an investment in the foundation that sustains and nurtures us throughout our lives. An essential aspect of this couple's success lies in their ability to forgive themselves and maintain good mental health. By practicing self-compassion and seeking help when it's needed, they've learned to navigate life's inevitable setbacks with resilience and grace.

Prioritizing mental health is not only vital for our well-being but also for the health and longevity of our relationships. Not too long ago, I had a client of mine, a very successful business owner, contact me and ask me for a referral to a therapist who specialized in entrepreneurs.

He had a very strong marriage but realized that as a business owner and entrepreneur, there were other challenges outside of his marriage that he wanted someone with experience to guide him through. I was grateful that I was able to connect him with an expert who could help him.

None of us is above having to ask for help – especially when it comes to mental health. There's something that is refreshing, and commendable about someone confident enough in themselves to ask for help. That realization of knowing "when" an acquired skill.

Society may have a negative stigma surrounding mental health issues, but we all have a need for help at different points in our lives. No one is immune.

Finally, the need for self-love cannot be overstated. Jared and Cherise's journey is a testament to the power of loving and accepting one's self. When we choose to embrace our authentic selves and cultivate self-love, we set the stage for healthier and more fulfilling relationships that enrich our lives and the lives of those around us.

In conclusion, the story of this successful couple serves as an inspiring reminder that our choices, communication and commitment to our loved ones and others pave the way to thriving and enduring relationships. By embracing the power of choice, prioritizing communication, choosing family first, forgiving ourselves and nurturing our mental health, we can unlock the secrets to living a successful life both in our relationships and beyond. Just ask Jared and Cherise.

Chapter 20

Reflecting on Life's Journeys: Choosing Paths and Partnerships

The story of Jared and Cherise Rodman is a compelling narrative that captures the essence of partnership, resilience, and the enduring power of family. It invites us as readers to reflect on the choices we make and the people we choose to journey with. Their experiences underscore the importance of aligning our actions with our deepest values and the strength found in true collaboration.

As we draw parallels between their story and our own lives, it's essential to take a step back and reflect upon the path that we're on. Let us use their insights as a catalyst for self-examination and a guide for better understanding our own relationships, career choices, and the intricate dance between personal aspirations and familial responsibilities.

Take some time to contemplate these questions. Let them stir your imagination, and don't hesitate to jot down your responses and the action items that come to mind. Your personal narrative is continually evolving, and with careful thought, you can shape it with intention and insight.

1. **Exploring Family Dynamics and Support:**
   - How have my family dynamics and the support I offer or receive within my family influenced my career choices and personal growth?
2. **Balancing Ambitions with Family Commitments:**
   - In what ways have I managed to balance my ambitions with my commitments to my family?

- What adjustments could better harmonize these two aspects of my life?

3. **Evaluating Risk and Opportunity:**
   - When faced with a risky opportunity, how do I evaluate its potential impact on my family?
   - What factors weigh most heavily in my decision-making process?

4. **Adapting to Unexpected Changes:**
   - How have I adapted to unexpected changes in my life?
   - What strategies have I used to maintain stability and well-being for myself and my loved ones?

5. **Defining Success on My Own Terms:**
   - How do I define success for myself?
   - In what ways does this definition align with my core values and the well-being of those closest to me?

The Rodmans' story is not just about navigating the complexities of life. It's about doing so with a shared vision and a united front. May their story inspire you to reflect upon your journey, cherish your partnerships, and approach each new chapter with courage and love.

Part 5

Jordan and
Adriane Erskine

Chapter 21

Jordan and Adriane Erskine Backstory

Not many relationships can be traced back to a visit with the orthodontist but that's exactly how it all started for the Erskines. Adriane was being fitted for braces and it was Jordan's sister-in-law who worked on her. One conversation led to another, and it wasn't long before a blind date was born – Jordan's first ever and only the second of Adriane's entire dating career.

Adriane laughs remembering how distraught her mother was over the whole idea. Neither of them knew who Jordan was and to make matters worse, Adriane didn't even know his last name! Her mom may not have been comfortable, but any reservations Adriane may have had melted away as soon as she opened that door. Adriane says she knew instantly that this was the man she was going to marry.

The relationship blossomed even though they both worked full-time and attended a local community college. According to Adriane, she didn't even want to be in school but felt pressure from her family. Her parents had come from Puerto Rico with nothing, so education was a priority in her home. After her parents divorced, she watched her mom work, put herself through college and raise a family all as a single mom. When her siblings followed in their mom's footsteps and put themselves through school, Adriane felt pressured to do the same.

The couple married and both earned their Bachelor's degree – Adriane in Human Resource Management and Jordan in Business Finance. Once Adriane graduated, they decided that Jordan would continue on to earn his Master's degree in International Business from Northeastern University in Boston.

He would be the first in his family to earn a college degree and although the price tag on his Master's degree would be in excess of $75,000, the couple felt that this was an important step for Jordan and their family. He completed his field studies in China and rushed back to Boston in time to walk with his class at graduation.

Both are grateful for their education. Adriane worked for 10 years in Human Resource Management and loved it. She considers the experience invaluable in learning how not to let her kids get away with anything! Although it's a chapter in her life that has come and gone, it's something she'd love to do again one day and something she feels she could easily return to.

Jordan took some great technical courses in college and learned a lot. However, he admits that no course could ever have taught him how to build a manufacturing business on a shoestring budget. That can only come from experience!

Jordan and Adriane work as a team. They have to because neither believe in doing anything halfway. Adriane takes care of three kids all under the age of seven while Jordan is an entrepreneur running not just one company, but actively involved in four different companies with the possibility of a fifth on the horizon.

Both are grateful for each other's contribution to their family. Jordan is the first to admit that Adriane's role in taking care of the kids is a full-time job and he couldn't possibly do what he does without her. Adriane admires his unwavering dedication to providing for his family.

Like most of the couples you've met in this book, family is a huge driver for Jordan and Adriane, and it hasn't always been easy. Not that long ago, they lived in a cramped townhome and were facing down $140,000 in student loan debt. They survived paycheck-to-paycheck, which Adriane admits was stressful and very challenging. During this time, they essentially gave up everything they wanted personally just to pay the bills and provide for the kids. This weighed heavily on Jordan as a young husband and father, but he would have worked three or four jobs if that's what was necessary to provide for his family.

Jordan works a lot, and he gives Adriane a lot of the credit for making that possible. He left what he describes as a "pretty cushy job" for a 2–3-year period of time when he wasn't making a lot of money. Jordan explained that if you have problems at home, it's virtually impossible to go to work 80 hours a week, start new businesses and handle all the stress that goes along with that.

She smiles as she recalls how many times he told her that she was "just going to have to trust him on this." At one point, he even shared a quote with her from William Green, *"The richest rewards go to those who resist the lure of instant gratification."*

Jordan never stopped believing in what was possible and Adriane never stopped believing in him. What she does at home allows him to continue to drive forward on a daily basis. Jordan credits her with being an amazing mom – she's always there for the kids teaching them the values they want to instill in their family. She's always there for him as well – providing the unconditional support he needs to be successful.

When he's stressed, he knows he doesn't have to worry about anything. She is his rock and always goes above and beyond. Jordan added that their relationship is so good that even when things do get strained, it doesn't affect them like it does some other couples. They know how important communication is. They talk a lot and always manage to work things out quickly.

The biggest challenge so far for them has been how much Jordan works. Although it's not as common as it once was, you'll still find him putting in a 20-hour day on occasion. He's started working a couple of days from home now, but Adriane is quick to point out that he is still working. If he's in the office, she knows he has work that must be done – even on nights and weekends.

Being an entrepreneur is not always easy on a family. When the kids were babies, a large part of their caregiving was taking care of basic physical needs and naturally fell to Adriane. Now that their first child is getting older, he's starting to notice how much Jordan is away and he wants more time with his dad. This has become an increasingly more challenging, emotional, balancing act for Adriane – one that will likely continue for quite some time.

When it comes to achieving huge success, having a strong and supportive spouse at home is not just a wish list item – something that would be nice to have. The role that Adriane and many other spouses of successful entrepreneurs play is an absolutely critical one. They must not only support the entrepreneur and keep them balanced through all of the uncertainty and stresses that go along with entrepreneurship, but they're also responsible for maintaining a happy and well-adjusted family life that makes success possible – and worthwhile.

Even with the fantastic success this couple has achieved, they remain humble. The blessing of where they are today and how far they've come is never lost on them. They have both worked very hard and are extremely grateful for all that they have accomplished.

Chapter 22

Jordan Erskine
Mindset

"Your mindset and perspective – when that's right – you kind of feel invincible. When you see some success – it becomes easier to see more success and what you could build and continue that cycle."

Jordan Erskine

Jordan is a serial entrepreneur – and a very good one at that. He has dedicated his entire career to the manufacturing industry and continues to prove that he has a gift for transforming his creative ideas into successful businesses.

With over 17 years of experience in the personal care/skin care industry, he cofounded Dynamic Blending with a friend of his in 2015. As President, Jordan has in many ways revolutionized the standard contract manufacturing business model. He eliminated large minimum order quantities and the exorbitant fees that were typical in the industry. He replaced them with an affordable turnkey solution for bringing cosmetics, skin care and personal care products to market. As a result, the company grew by over 11,500% in less than 4 years. Jordan is now considered a business innovator by many in the industry.

He has built quite an extensive resume in a very short period of time. In addition to Dynamic Blending, Jordan is also a cofounder of NarcX Solutions, a company that uses environmentally compliant processes to provide safe drug disposal of opioids onsite. He is also cofounder of VivaRed Supplements and ProcureMe – a global supply chain and logistics company. He is the lead investor in a company called Launch Fulfillment – a third-party freight logistics and fulfillment company and the founding partner of Red Giant Ventures -an angel investment firm.

Defining Success

Success obviously means different things to different people. To Jordan, success is having the ability to spend more time with his family. With a work schedule that includes 20-hour days on a regular basis, he hasn't been able to take the kids on weekend outings as much as he would have liked.

He continues to build a network of project teams at Dynamic Blending in hopes of being able to step away more in the future. Although he has started working more from home, he hopes to reach a point where he won't have to be on the job until 2:00 or 3:00 in the morning anymore. He wants the next success chapter in his life centered around his kids and spending more time with them as they grow up.

In this day and age, Jordan says you can't *not* think about money. It's his dream to build generational wealth. Family is a key driver for Jordan, and he always wants to be in a position to help not just their kids but also the couple's parents. He wants to have the opportunity to give back, donate money and do all the "cool stuff" you can't do without money.

Jordan is a man who never takes his success lightly. He is cognizant every day of the many people who depend on the decisions he makes. He understands that the ripple effects that his decisions have are huge – not just for his family, but for his employees, customers, and everyone they touch.

A top personal goal of Jordan's was to get the family's home paid off. Once he checked that item off his list, he said that he feels as though a giant 747 has been lifted from his shoulders. The house is no longer tied to anything and in his mind, that equates to more time and flexibility with less stress and pressure!

Lessons Learned

When I asked Jordan about the greatest lessons learned so far on this journey, he smiled and said it would have to be learning to slow down enough to enjoy the journey. He believes that the path they're on is unique and not everyone has been given the opportunities that they have. He wants to remember daily just how blessed he is and how amazing their journey has been.

If he had to do it all over again – would he have done anything differently? According to Jordan, not much. He admits that with each company he's become a little wiser. The only area that he admits he would have done things differently concerned some of the partners he brought in early and the equity he gave them.

In the beginning, when you're bootstrapping a company, there's typically not a lot of money coming in, but you still need capital and talent. In many cases, the only way you have to pay talent is with equity. A common pitfall among new entrepreneurs is giving away too much of the company before you ever get started. In hindsight, Jordan says he would have probably structured things a little differently in the early days in terms of compensation.

The Next Generation

Of all the lessons he'd like to pass along to his kids, the greatest one would be the value of hard work. It's no secret that Jordan works hard. He would like his kids to not only establish a strong work ethic, but he'd like them to always strive to do their best work every time. Everyday try to be better than yesterday.

He shared that when he was growing up, his dad worked two or three jobs on the side, and no one ever heard him complain. He never had the opportunity to earn a college degree, but Jordan still remembers all the wonderful vacations his father took the family on when he was growing up. Jordan's relentless drive to take care of his family may actually in part come from his dad.

It's important to this couple that their kids remain grounded and understand what's most important in life. Jordan says that he's personally witnessed far too many people ruining their lives just so they can drive a BMW. That's not the life he wants for his children.

When he looks back on where they began relative to where they are now, he believes that there was obviously a higher power involved. He wants to instill the values of family, faith and prayer into their kids from a young age.

Jordan believes a sign of the times is more people seem less willing to help others. He wants to teach his kids to enjoy giving back and helping others. It's important to him that they understand just how fortunate they are and are grateful for all the opportunities they have been given.

Jordan continues to take a lot on. That's just who he is. The kids aren't slowing down anytime soon, and he still doesn't have an executive assistant, but he and Adriane make it work. She is his rock, and he is committed to taking care of his family. They are a team.

Chapter 23

Adriane Erskine
Mental Health

"Therapy saved my life. What started as postpartum anxiety, became healing from childhood which moved into learning to become a better wife and mom by healing me. I feel like everyone would benefit from therapy."

Adriane Erskine

A driane admits that when she married Jordan, she never imagined that their life would grow into what it is today. In those early years, her definition of success was simple. Success meant graduating with their degrees and landing decent enough jobs that they could pay their bills.

Now that they've achieved some financial stability – success revolves much more around quality time with family. They'd like to eventually buy a second home away from the city so they can pack the family up and escape for the weekends.

Although Jordan takes most Fridays off from the office now, he's still always working from home – nights, weekends and often until the wee hours of the morning. Adriane dreams of a day when time off from the office means actual time off for her husband. She worries about Jordan and that he doesn't take enough time for himself – time he needs to rejuvenate and keep going with his grueling schedule.

Consistency and Discipline

When I asked Adriane what words would best describe their journey so far, she replied without hesitation – consistency and discipline. She said it all starts with knowing and understanding what success means to your family and to you personally. From there, a dream is born. Then it's up to you to believe in your dream and have the courage to reach for it consistently and with discipline on a daily basis.

She was quick to add that this is not always easy. In fact, sometimes it can be tough – even grueling and miserable at times. However, they work at it consistently day in and day out because they know if they just keep going – all their work and sacrifices will pay off.

Adriane believes that it's vitally important that you feed your dreams hope and take the time to see little glimpses of success along the way. It's been said that the days are long, but the years are short. Without these glimpses of what the future can hold, it would be virtually impossible to get up and do the same thing over and over every day.

She's quick to point out that you can sometimes find these glimpses in the smallest and simplest of things. You don't need an extravagant vacation to see them. Adriane shared that her kids love the sporting goods store, Scheels. Sometimes, they'll grab lunch and just walk around Scheels with the kids for a little while before heading home. Other times, it can be as simple as making sandwiches and having dinner in the park or flying kites together.

What's most important according to Adriane is that you're intentional about setting these up or chances are, they will never happen. Both Jordan and Adriane have input on these special times but the planning falls to Adriane and she doesn't mind at all. She feels like this is something she can do for Jordan. She knows him well enough to know that if he had to try to plan these outings in between everything else he does in a day, it would add stress and detract from his enjoyment.

The couple is always sensitive to what's possible for their kids at their age. These times are too precious to the family, to plan something the kids won't enjoy and will complain about the entire time.

If consistency and discipline describe their journey so far, it's these little glimpses of success that keep them going on their path. Jordan makes them possible in his role and Adriane makes them happen in hers. It gives them time to pause, enjoy and remember why they both work as hard as they do for their family.

The Right Support Team

On life's journeys, it's important that you feel you're not alone. Surrounding yourself with the right support team is essential to the success of every entrepreneur. The same is true of the successful entrepreneur's spouse. For Adriane, that team consists of Jordan, of course, their parents, her therapist, a couple of close friends and a wonderful lady who helps Adriane around the house and with the kids once a week.

She admits that she is meticulous in choosing who she allows in this group. She holds a great deal of respect for everyone on her support team and feels that same level of respect back from them. These are all people she knows she can count on.

Although everyone on her team supports Adriane in different ways at different times, the help she receives with the kids from their parents is priceless. Jordan's mom dedicates one of her days every single week to just being with the kids which gives Adriane time to get out of the house, breathe and run errands. One night a month, she has all the grandkids over to spend the night which is something everyone looks forward to – kids and adults alike!

Adriane's mom is always there to help as well. Recently, one of the kids had strep throat. Her mom came over immediately to watch the other kids while Adriane took her sick child to the doctor. Adriane loves having that time and connection with her mom. After all, her mom raised three kids on her own so she knows just how challenging it can be sometimes.

One of the close friends on Adriane's team is married to an entrepreneur and knows all about the unique challenges that go along with that. They both feel very fortunate that they have each other to talk to.

Mental Health

When an individual decides to see a therapist, it doesn't mean that there's anything wrong with the person or with their marriage. Adriane is very open and proud of the work that she's done in therapy. She views therapy as a tool for learning to heal, stretch and grow in life.

There is no doubt in Adriane's mind that she would not be the person she is today without professional counseling. In many ways, she credits her therapist with actually saving her life.

Adriane suffered from severe postpartum anxiety. She felt confused and depressed because she knew something was wrong but had no idea what it was. Without help, it was only a matter of time before her condition would begin to affect her marriage and her ability to parent. She wanted to do everything in her power to avoid that – so she found a therapist.

Over time, her therapy has become a healing process from childhood and working through past traumas. She soon discovered that healing things within herself was her path to becoming a better wife and mother.

She now compares her mental health and well-being to a puzzle containing many different pieces. To continue to evolve into the person she wants to be, those pieces must all fit together just right.

Another insight Adriane gained through therapy was the realization that she wasn't alone, and she didn't have to figure everything out on her own. Other people understood the pain she was feeling and wanted to help her understand and move through the issues that held her back.

Adriane also believes that the couple's communication has improved as a result of therapy. Open communication takes work. Although they both recognized this skill as a critical component in the success of their marriage, family, and dreams, it didn't always come naturally to them. She and Jordan are now able to communicate their needs and desires much more openly.

Built into the entrepreneurial spirit is a willingness to be vulnerable in order to achieve your hopes and dreams. With the help of therapy, this couple now feels that they are both doing everything they can to not only make that happen but to also make it easier on one another. That's the beauty of their team.

Lessons Learned

When I asked Adriane about the greatest lessons that she's learned so far on her journey, she was silent for a moment. Then, with tears in her eyes she whispered that life doesn't stop. Remember to take in what's right in front of you right in that moment. She continued that it's not always about looking forward and to what's next.

She feels it's so important to sometimes take a step back and appreciate what's really going on. The kids will only be little once. Before you know it, they'll be grown and gone. She doesn't want to miss that, and she doesn't want Jordan to miss it either.

She confided that sometimes when Jordan comes home all excited about a new business idea, she can't help but look at him in disbelief. Although she's never told him no, she sometimes wonders why it always has to be go, go, go. A lesson she feels they should never forget is to look at what's right in front of them right at the moment and embrace that.

Another lesson that Adriane feels is so important to always remember is that you're not alone. There's great value in someone saying that they know what it feels like. She believes that there's great comfort and strength that comes from knowing that – so much so, that she actually reached out to my wife at our first book signing.

She shared that she felt such an emotional pull to her that she wanted to give her a big hug. She said that she knew exactly what my wife has been through supporting me in my career and as I've worked on this book. It meant the world to my wife, and I think it means the world to other entrepreneur spouses when someone can reinforce that they are *not* alone and someone else knows and has experienced some of the challenges they face.

Lessons Learned From Jordan and Adriane

In the labyrinth of life, when business dynamics intertwine with personal aspirations, often, it's the relationships that bear the weight of all of the sacrifices, silent victories, and whispered dreams it took to get there. The Erskine's tale is a testament to this sentiment. Jordan and Adriane's journey is not merely about building successful enterprises. It's more about fostering a life built on trust, understanding, and a shared vision of success.

Throughout this book, we've dissected the intricacies of managing businesses, the challenges of entrepreneurship, and the delicate balance between personal and professional life. What stands out to me time and time again in each story I've shared, is the silent resilience of the spouse behind the scenes – the Adriane to every Jordan. Too many times, the spouse's perspective is overshadowed by the glitz of business achievements. Yet, it remains the bedrock upon which entrepreneurial dreams are built and sustained.

It's easy to be swept up in the stories of successful businesses – their exponential growth rates, and revolutionary innovations are the envy of competitors. However, what often goes unspoken is the personal cost - the long hours, the missed family dinners, and the emotional toll left in the wake of an entrepreneur's relentless pursuit of success. This book serves as a reminder that for every entrepreneur pushing boundaries, there is a supportive partner, a family and a world that operates behind the scenes silently making sacrifices and standing as the unwavering pillar of strength.

The story of Jordan's rise from a community college student to a business magnate is undeniably inspiring. Yet, equally as compelling is Adriane's journey from managing the chaos of home, kids, and her personal challenges, to remaining Jordan's anchor regardless of what's happening around them. Her tale shines a light on all of the unsung heroes in the lives of entrepreneurs.

Adriane's insights into mental health also underline a pivotal message for business owners and their spouses. While ambition drives us forward, self-awareness and self-care are essential to never losing ourselves in the process. Her brave disclosure about therapy serves as a beacon for many who silently grapple with their inner challenges. Adriane is living proof that seeking help is a strength, not a weakness.

Jordan's perspective on success, his aspiration to build generational wealth while ensuring quality time with family, resonates with entrepreneurs around the world. It's a reflection of the contemporary entrepreneur mindset – one where success isn't defined exclusively by financial milestones but rather, by the legacy one leaves behind, both personally and professionally.

For many readers – especially those navigating the turbulent waters of entrepreneurship and relationships, the Erskines offer a roadmap. They epitomize the idea that while the journey may be filled with hurdles – with the right partner, communication, and shared values, it is possible to chart a path that balances personal happiness and professional achievement.

In closing, the Erskines' story is not just one of financial strategies and business acumen. It's one of understanding the profound interplay between relationships, mental well-being, and ambition. Jordan and Adriane, in their unique way, teach us that success is a collective endeavor – one in which personal relationships are as critical, if not more so, than business strategies.

To all business owners and their spouses: Your journey, with its ups and downs, is a testament to the human spirit's resilience and ability to dream. As you navigate through every page of your entrepreneurial story, remember to cherish and nurture the silent pillars that hold your world together. For in them lies the true essence of success.

Chapter 25

Reflecting on Life's Journeys: The Partnership of Dreams and Reality

As we conclude the chapters detailing Jordan and Adriane Erskine's journey, we find a narrative replete with shared dreams, a steadfast partnership, and the continuous interplay between ambition and familial devotion. Their story is a testament to the belief that success is not a solo endeavor but rather a duet sung in harmony with those we hold dear. In this dance of life, each step taken is measured not only by the stride toward our goals but also by the warmth of the hands we hold along the way.

Before we venture into the questions that might help us map our paths, let us pause and reflect. Consider the roads you have traveled, the decisions that have defined your journey, and the partnerships that have supported your strides.

Take a moment to consider these questions, and as insights surface, allow yourself to sketch out the action items they inspire. It is in these reflections that we chart the course for tomorrow's dreams.

1. **Assessing the Role of Education and Opportunity:**
   - How has my educational journey shaped my current path?
   - In what ways have I leveraged or diverged from that path in pursuit of my aspirations?
2. **Understanding Sacrifices in Partnership:**
   - What sacrifices have my partner and I made to support each other's goals?
   - How do we navigate the balance between individual aspirations and our shared life?
3. **Evaluating the Influence of Family Background:**

- In what ways has my family background influenced my definition of success?
- How have I honored or redefined that influence in my personal and professional life?

4. **Recognizing and Handling Financial Pressures:**
   - How have financial pressures shaped my relationship with my partner?
   - What strategies have we employed to manage stress and maintain a supportive environment?

5. **Defining Success Beyond Monetary Gains:**
   - Beyond monetary success, how do I define a fulfilling life?
   - What steps am I taking to ensure that my definition of success encompasses personal well-being and family happiness?

As you reflect upon these questions, remember that life's journey is seldom a straight line. Often, it's those curves in the road that lead to unexpected and amazing vistas. May the story of the Erskines inspire you to embrace your journey with courage, to value your partnerships, and to always remember that success is sweetest when shared.

Conclusion: Envisioning a Life of Significance

In my unique role as a wealth manager, I've had the profound honor of guiding clients not merely to financial success but to their vision of a life of significance. What drives me, what our firm is renowned for, is empowering you to create a life that resonates deeply with your values—one that transcends the ordinary and touches on the extraordinary.

The stories in this book are not just stories. They are life lessons from the front lines of success – where triumph often emerges from the ashes of setbacks. Our clients – affluent families with substantial financial success, are now on a quest to craft a legacy of significance, both for themselves and for the loved ones they hold dear.

I've distilled their wisdom into five vital lessons that from my experience are the essential pillars that support a life of true significance:

Resilience: The Pulse of Triumph

The families I've had the privilege to work with understand that their success is not a twist of fate but the result of unyielding resilience. They've taught us that enduring strength to persevere is what forges a legacy worth remembering.

Vision: A Canvas of Intention

True success isn't stumbled upon; it is deliberately designed. It's about seizing the artist's brush and painting the masterpiece of your life with strokes of intention and purpose.

Wealth: A Catalyst for Purpose

As I walk alongside these families, I've witnessed wealth transform from a measure of success to a catalyst for living a life filled with passion, purpose, and deep personal fulfillment.

Synergy: The Path Forged With Intention

At the heart of their success lies the synergy between their aspirations and my guidance. Together, we align their financial resources with their most cherished dreams, ensuring a harmonious journey towards a horizon rich with significance.

Partnership: The Voyage Beyond Numbers

The essence of my role extends beyond mere numbers. It is about being a steadfast companion on their lifelong journey, navigating through the ebbs and flows, and charting a course towards a life replete with moments that truly matter.

As I reflect on my profession, the greatest joy comes not from managing wealth but from immersing myself in the dreams of those I serve. It's about standing shoulder-to-shoulder with families and guiding them as they navigate the crossroads of their lives. It's about helping them to chart a course toward the future they envision, and planning the active steps necessary to manifest it.

This book is a tribute to the quiet strength and enduring spirit of these families. It challenges the preconceived notions of success, revealing that it is not merely the accumulation of wealth, but the richness of a life lived with unwavering intention, boundless love, and a steadfast pursuit of what genuinely matters.

In closing, may the tapestry of these stories inspire you to forge your own path of meaningful achievements. Remember, wealth is merely the enabler, and the true architect of success is you—armed with clarity, intention, and a vision for the life of significance you are destined to live.

ABOUT THE AUTHOR

Born and raised in American Fork, UT, Rob and his wife, Melissa, chose to raise their three children in the same hometown that shaped his own upbringing. Family is their top priority, and they cherish every moment together. Their family activities range from camping and playing sports, to pool parties, taking vacations and working in their garden together.

Rob's upbringing instilled in him the importance of hard work, integrity, service, leadership, and strong personal relationships. This laid the foundation for his achievements in both his professional career and public service.

These core values led him to establish Axio Wealth Management, a financial advisory firm that specializes in wealth management with a deeper mission: empowering successful families to unlock the freedom to live their best life. This ethos, central to Axio Wealth Management, drives their dedication to guiding families toward financial freedom and a fulfilling lifestyle.

Rob is the published author of two insightful books aimed at helping families achieve financial security and resilience. His first book, *Is My Family Going To Be Okay? What Successful Families Do To Answer That Question* guides families in preparing for unexpected life events. His second book, *From Together To Triumph* explores different strategies for family success. These works highlight his commitment to financial education and empowerment.

Rob's passion for his community shines through his active involvement and commitment to giving back. He currently serves as treasurer for the Make-A-Wish Utah executive board. He has also held significant roles in various local organizations including: the American Fork City Council, Central Utah Dispatch, North Pointe Sold Waste, Utah Valley Estate Planning Council as Vice-President, and the Utah Valley Chamber policy committee.

Rob attended Utah Valley University and Western Governor's University where he earned a degree in Finance. For over 20 years, he has dedicated his talents and knowledge to the field of wealth management and financial planning. Rob is the founder of Axio Wealth Management.

Made in the USA
Columbia, SC
06 June 2024

36584608R00129